Secrets
to
Success
for
Social Studies
Teachers

Secrets to Success for Social Studies Teachers

Ellen Kottler
Nancy P. Gallavan

CORWIN PRESS
A SAGE Publications Company
Thousand Oaks, CA 91320

For information:

Corwin Press
A Sage Publications Company
2455 Teller Road
Thousand Oaks,
    California 91320
www.corwinpress.com

Sage Publications India Pvt. Ltd.
B 1/I 1 Mohan Cooperative
    Industrial Area
Mathura Road, New Delhi 110 044
India

Sage Publications Ltd.
1 Oliver's Yard
55 City Road
London EC1Y 1SP
United Kingdom

Sage Publications Asia-Pacific Pte. Ltd.
33 Pekin Street #02-01
Far East Square
Singapore 048763

Printed in the United States of America

Library of Congress Cataloging-in-Publication Data

Kottler, Ellen.
Secrets to success for social studies teachers/Ellen Kottler, Nancy P. Gallavan
    p. cm.
Includes bibliographical references and index.
ISBN 978-1-4129-5026-8 (cloth)
ISBN 978-1-4129-5027-5 (paperback)
    1. Social sciences—Study and teaching (Middle School)—United States. 2. Social sciences—Study and teaching (Secondary)—United States. 3. First year teachers—Training of—United States. 4. Teacher orientation—United States. I. Gallavan, Nancy P. II. Title.

H62.5.U5K68 2008
300.71'273—dc22   2007008783

This book is printed on acid-free paper.

07   08   09   10   11   10   9   8   7   6   5   4   3   2   1

Acquisitions Editor:	Rachel Livsey
Managing Editor:	Jessica Allan
Editorial Assistants:	Phyllis Cappello, Joanna Coelho
Production Editor:	Astrid Virding
Copy Editor:	Jovey Stewart
Typesetter:	C&M Digitals (P) Ltd.
Proofreader:	Ellen Brink
Indexer:	Molly Hall
Cover Designer:	Michael Dubowe
Graphic Designer:	Lisa Miller

Contents

Foreword

At one time, a book like this would not be needed by beginning social studies teachers. It was believed that a new social studies teacher was the same as a new teacher in any other field. In most districts, social studies teachers received the same basic preparation as every other new teacher. They went to workshops alongside their colleagues from other disciplines and learned about bulletin boards, classroom management, school policies and the like.

For many new social studies teachers, their preservice preparation in teaching was also similar to that of their colleagues, despite the differences in coursework outside the College of Education. I know of teacher education programs that required the same general methods course for everyone, whether the candidate was preparing for first grade or twelfth, for social studies or science, even for music, art, and physical education.

The belief that "teaching is teaching" was weakened when Lee Shulman and his associates at Stanford University discovered that effective teachers in different subject areas used distinctly different techniques. The concept of "pedagogical content knowledge" was born. Universities and school systems began to differentiate between teachers by subject area instead of having them participate in common courses and staff development sessions.

A related trend was the development of subject area supervisors in larger school districts. These educational leaders were responsible for the staff development of teachers under their supervision. After all, one could no longer expect a principal with a background in mathematics to help a social studies teacher with pedagogical content knowledge any more than a social studies supervisor could advise a dance teacher.

Supervisors in social studies became instrumental in the growth and development of teachers in their districts. In addition to providing relevant in-service programs and resources, the supervisors encouraged and arranged for teachers to join their state and local social studies councils, attend social studies conferences, and subscribe to the leading professional journals in the field. Supervisors were especially crucial in promoting attendance at the annual meeting of the prestigious National Council for the Social Studies (NCSS), Indeed, the supervisors formed their own Associated Group at NCSS, called NSSSA—the National Social Studies Supervisors Association.

This rather sensible system was dealt a blow by the passage of No Child Left Behind in 2001. The new law placed such an enormous emphasis on improving test scores in mathematics and literacy that school districts began to cut back on their commitment to in-service training that was specifically designed for social studies teachers. There was less money for social studies membership and conference attendance, and less support for social studies supervisors. Many districts replaced social studies supervisors with general ones, who tended to emphasize literacy goals.

So, we've come full circle. Social studies teachers will certainly benefit from in-service training regarding literacy, but they will miss out on the knowledge and skills that are specifically relevant to their teaching assignments. New teachers can compensate by joining the National Council for the Social Studies along with their state councils and also by studying the book that you hold in your hands. New teachers, indeed all teachers, need a handbook to guide them in their work. This book holds a valuable place in every social studies teacher's professional library.

Jeff Passe
Professor of Reading and Elementary Education
University of North Carolina at Charlotte
President, National Council for the Social Studies, 2005–2006

Acknowledgments

The authors would like to thank their colleagues, mentors, students, teachers, and the young learners who contributed their insights and inspiration and to extend their appreciation to Rachel Livsey for her support of this project. Ellen thanks her husband Jeffrey and son Cary for their support. Nancy heartily thanks her husband Richard for his encouraging interest and continuous care, her colleagues Kathy and Diane, and especially her coauthor Ellen for their dynamic conversations related to the social sciences.

The contributions of the following reviewers are gratefully acknowledged:

Peggy Altoff
Coordinator of Social Studies, K–12
Colorado Springs School District 11
Colorado Springs, Colo.

Steve Armstrong
Social Studies Department Supervisor
West Hartford Public Schools
West Hartford, Conn.

John Lee
Associate Professor
Curriculum, Instruction & Counselor Education
North Carolina State University
Raleigh, N.C.

David L. Moguel
Associate Professor
Secondary Education Department
Michael D. Eisner College of Education
California State University, Northridge
Northridge, Calif.

Paul Nagel
Coordinator, Louisiana Geography Education Alliance
College of Education
Northwestern State University
Natchitoches, La.

About the Authors

 **Ellen Kottler** received her bachelor's degree from the University of Michigan, her master's degree from Eastern Michigan University, and her EdS from the University of Nevada, Las Vegas. She was a secondary school teacher for over twenty-five years in public, private, and alternative school settings. She also served as an administrative specialist in curriculum and professional development for the Clark County School District (Las Vegas). She is active in the National Council for the Social Studies. She is author or coauthor of journal articles and books for educators, including *Secrets to Success for Beginning Elementary School Teachers* (2007), *Counseling Skills for Teachers* (2007), *On Being a Teacher: The Human Dimension* (2005), *Secrets for Secondary School Teachers: How to Succeed in Your First Year* (2004), and *Children With Limited English: Teaching Strategies for the Regular Classroom* (2002).

Ellen currently is a lecturer in the College of Education at California State University, Fullerton, and a grant writer for the Anaheim Union High School District (Anaheim, California).

 **Nancy P. Gallavan** worked as an elementary and middle school teacher in the St. Vrain Valley and Cherry Creek School Districts of Colorado for twenty years while earning her master's degree from the University of Colorado and her PhD from the University of Denver. Prior to her current position, she was an associate professor of teacher education specializing in social studies and multicultural education at the University of Nevada, Las Vegas. Nancy has authored more than sixty publications including books, chapters, and articles in professional education journals including *Secrets to*

Success for Beginning Elementary School Teachers (2007) and *What Prinicipals Need to Know About Teaching Social Studies* (2003). She is active in the Association of Teacher Education (ATE), the National Association for Multicultural Education (NAME), and the National Council for the Social Studies (NCSS).

Nancy currently is a professor of teacher education and the Associate Dean of the College of Education at the University of Central Arkansas.

Introduction

Wow! Look at this curriculum! How can I be sure all my students are actively engaged in powerful social studies learning and score well on the tests? What do I do to create a strong community of learners and independent problem solvers? Where will I find primary sources and teaching materials to make the learning meaningful for my students? These are just a few of the many questions most social studies teachers ask everyday.

Welcome to the world of social studies education. To help you gather the answers to these and other questions, we share this book filled with a wealth of practical, easy-to-implement, and creative ideas. We have written this book for all social studies educators, scattering indispensable secrets throughout the book to help ensure your success. You include middle-level teachers, middle school and junior high school teachers, and high school teachers. You teach courses in general social studies; in core areas, such as civics or government, economics, geography, and history; or in non-core areas, such as psychology, sociology, and anthropology, to name a few. Each course is developed for a specific grade level and type of learner, such as state government for English learners or Advanced Placement Economics for college-bound high school juniors and seniors. This book will be a valuable resource for all classroom teachers seeking guidance and support to improve their own social studies teaching.

This book also will be a useful tool for department chairs and curriculum specialists as they mentor novice and experienced teachers and advance their own professional growth and development. In addition, the concepts and practices presented in this book will benefit school administrators and teacher educators who guide and/or supervise social studies teachers.

The book is divided into twelve chapters, each with pragmatic guidelines, checklists, and resources: secrets to ensure immediate success.

Chapter 1 begins with a discussion of the social studies classroom as you orient yourself for your particular teaching assignment and create a community of learners.

Chapter 2 introduces social studies as a discipline and guides you through state standards, district expectations, and your school's mission in developing your curriculum.

Chapter 3 focuses on meaningful instruction to engage and empower your students.

Chapters 4 and 5 help you strengthen outcomes by aligning curriculum and instruction with assessment, connecting social studies skills and learning with your students' lives.

Chapter 6 examines the integration of literacy skills, using the textbook as a tool to build social studies skills.

Chapter 7 addresses meaningful instruction by knowing your students, identifying important concepts, selecting your themes and units, and planning significant learning experiences to make the most of your time and your students' interests and energies.

Chapter 8 suggests ways to collaborate with colleagues through teaching teams, departments, and other school personnel.

Chapter 9 describes how to incorporate a variety of resources, including artifacts, teaching trunks, videos, slide presentations, guest speakers, and field trips.

Chapter 10 covers the use of instructional technology in the classroom and features a rich reference list of Web sites organized by subject area.

Chapter 11 suggests a wide range of supplementary activities to enrich and enhance learning listed by subject area.

Finally, Chapter 12 encourages teachers to reflect on their practices and plan for future professional development.

We invite each of you to tailor this book to your own unique situation. As we address a broad range of topics and issues relevant for many different types of social studies educators, we encourage you to customize and extend the information within each chapter so the suggestions apply appropriately to your needs and wants. We think you will soon discover that the entire book offers innovative and productive ideas that will help you become more competent, confident, and ready as a social studies teacher.

CHAPTER ONE

Design Your Classroom to Create Communities of Learners

How exciting! You have been given your teaching assignment and handed the key to a classroom. Now it is time to use your knowledge, skills, and experience to create a community of learners. Your first task is to set the stage for effective teaching and learning every day in your own social studies classroom.

EXPLORE YOUR SCHOOL AND CLASSROOM

Take a tour and see your school in action. As you walk around the building, take note of the layout and activities. Consider these questions: Are classrooms grouped by department or grade level? Do students enter from the outside or from an inside hallway? What types of projects do you see students engaged in, especially in the social studies classes? How and where do teachers obtain books and supplies? Where is your room located in relation to the other school facilities?

1

Here are some items you want to see and discuss with your colleagues to be prepared for the first day of school:

- Location of the main office, health office, restrooms, and lunchroom
- Location of the media center and technology labs
- Copy of the school district teacher handbook and curriculum guide
- Copy of the student handbook
- List of your tentatively assigned grade levels and courses
- List of your assigned students noted with special needs (including learning, social, family, and health needs)
- Copies of the course textbooks and syllabi
- Location of your classroom (or rooms if you will be a traveling teacher)
- Types of student desks or tables and chairs assigned to your classroom
- Availability of bulletin boards and display spaces in your classroom
- Availability of technology and storage areas within your classroom
- Location of your team/department office or planning room and storage areas
- Copies of the school calendar and schedule with the first day of work and the first day of school for students
- Directions to preferred places to park your car and whether or not a permit is required
- Directions to the faculty lounge and restrooms

As you become acquainted with each of these items, you will generate more questions and begin to plan for your students. This "preview of coming attractions" will help you get centered and enhance your peace of mind about your career as a social studies teacher. We will discuss these items in much more detail throughout the upcoming chapters.

MEET YOUR DEPARTMENT AND TEAM

You are going to spend most of your school time outside of your classroom with your department or team members. Although you might have been hired to teach specific social studies courses, you also were hired to fit into a particular group of people. Most teams want you to be an individual who successfully balances working on your own with working with others. You may be sharing students with other teachers; you may be team teaching with other teachers. You may work together to develop lesson plans and benchmark assessments. Every teacher will contribute to both your immediate effectiveness and long term success in some way. And every teacher will have more or different experiences than you bring to share with you. Our first secret for success is for you to learn from each person's strengths and expertise as you refine your skills and independence.

Many schools are organized into grade levels or academic departments with a group leader known as a department chair. Department chairs usually have been teaching at their schools a long time. They will likely be the ones to help you get your course textbooks, supplementary materials, and classroom supplies. Sometimes department chairs determine course assignments and periods taught. They can usually link you to professional organizations and professional development opportunities too.

INVESTIGATE YOUR SCHOOL HISTORY AND CUSTOMS

Schools are institutions frequently named for individuals who may be famous nationally or well known locally. Sometimes the namesake is still living, visits the school, and makes donations. It is exciting when you and your students meet the person for whom your school is named and learn what contributions this person made to the community to receive this special recognition.

Investigate your school's background. Frequently there are trophy cases, wall plaques, and group photographs displayed throughout the building. The annual yearbooks may be housed in the library. If you ask about your school in the faculty lounge or department planning room, it is likely someone will be happy to share stories of the school's history. It is both fun and informative to find out more about your school. Also, you can use these resources as ways of connecting your students to social studies with an immediate historical or sociological perspective. Discuss the significance of collecting and displaying local artifacts with your students. Take a field trip in your own school! Your school also functions around a set of customs and traditions (Cattani, 2002). By watching and listening carefully, you will realize how to promote and replicate the accepted ways of doing things at your new school. You will learn who is responsible for various aspects of the school's operations, how teachers and administrators expect you and your students to behave, and so forth. These are excellent topics to discuss with your department chair, team members, and/or a mentor.

Another secret is to use school customs and traditions as topics in your classroom. Have students discuss active citizenship, analyze roles and norms, or investigate group behaviors. Help students become aware of their school culture.

ACCESS TEXTBOOKS AND EQUIPMENT

When you obtain copies of your course textbooks and sample syllabi, you can begin reading them to prepare for the coming school year. Also ask for the teacher's manuals and supplementary teaching materials that either accompany the books or that have been purchased for your courses. Yet, be aware that teaching assignments may change during the summer or even in the beginning of the school year as the student population and faculty commitments stabilize.

Take inventory of the various kinds of teaching equipment and resources that are available. See what types of realia, primary source documents, and teaching models your school possesses. Inquire if there is a catalogue of your school's video and software collections. The types of equipment you can easily access certainly will impact the ways that you plan and implement your teaching strategies and learning experiences. Then, begin a wish list of items you would like to obtain when there is money available in the school budget. Check to see if your district has equipment standards for social studies classrooms. (See Box 1.1)

PLAN FOR DESKS AND DISPLAYS

I like the teacher to be in the front with the students around the teacher in a semicircle. The teacher walks around class and talks to students.

Atul, age 15, Grade 10

Box 1.1   Social Studies Materials and Equipment

- Atlases
- Cultural artifacts
- Globes
- Flags
- Historic costumes
- Maps: current and historical
- Display cases
- Chalkboards or whiteboards
- Smart Board
- Overhead and/or ELMO or other electric imaging projector
- Television
- DVD, CD, and/or videotape player(s)
- Computer(s)—desktop or laptop
- Printer
- Scanner
- Internet connections for one or more computers
- Large screen for projections

The classroom environment sets the tone for your students (Kottler, Kottler, & Kottler, 2004). You want your room to be both attractive and functional. It should be a place where students feel welcome, safe, and comfortable. Post your name and room number near the door. If possible, place a social studies poster on or beside the door that indicates the subjects taught in your room.

> *When a teacher puts up posters that he or she likes, the students that come into the classroom can get a basic idea of what kind of person their new teacher might be.*
>
> Trent, age 14, Grade 9

First, imagine what your students as well as other visitors will see as they enter. Display social studies materials and objects in this space. You can use maps, globes, models, time lines, posters, books, artifacts, and so forth. Over time, change your exhibits to reflect the topics and issues that you are studying in your courses to stimulate new ideas. Display products created by your students. Your goal is to captivate your students' interests and to communicate that engaging, challenging, and rewarding social studies education will be happening in your classroom.

Second, arrange the desks and furniture to allow students to move around the room quickly and easily; they need to be able to see you and the boards without any obstructions. Position the desks or tables into groups, half circles or circles, or a horseshoe shape to offer the most effective learning environments for your activities. Seating arrangements reflect your teaching styles. You want students to interact with one another and to work in collaborative learning groups. Sitting at tables or desks grouped in fours can facilitate these activities readily.

From a new teacher: "*My classroom is set up in a way that works for me. I have the students divided into two groups. Debates are a frequent occurrence in my classroom so this set-up works the best for me. It saves some time, which can be added to the instructional time for the students. It is also a nice set-up when playing review games prior to tests.*"

Third, determine where you will place three-dimensional items, such as artifacts and models. Some objects you will let students handle, while others may be fragile and personal and you will want students to only look at them. Strategically place bookshelves, side tables, and/or display cases within students' view. Then move other furniture, such as wardrobes and file cabinets, to the walls or corners where students can access them for books, materials, and supplies, so you can see all parts of the room. You may have to make accommodations if your classroom is small, the seating is fixed, or other furniture is immovable.

Fourth, consider where to place your desk. Some teachers want their desks placed near the door; some teachers want their desks placed near the front of the classroom, which is usually where the boards are located. Yet, some teachers want their desks placed near the back of the classroom. Each location has benefits and limitations, and each teacher is unique. We suggest that you walk through other teachers' classrooms to see how they have arranged their classrooms. You might want to match them since it will be the configuration that the students will expect. Or you might want to be different to capture your students' attention and signal what activities they will engage in while in social studies.

Fifth, dedicate distinct portions of your walls to highlight each course that you will be teaching. Save one space for general information. Use bulletin boards or cork strips to post reference information and related articles from newspapers, magazines, and journals. Set aside a special area to recognize student work. Here are two extremely important secrets: Find ways to display samples of every student's work from all your courses, and rotate the student work regularly throughout the school year. We also encourage you, from the first day of school, to display emergency procedures near the door and prepare everyone for all types of emergencies and evacuation. (See Box 1.2)

Box 1.2   Materials and Purposes for Social Studies Bulletin Board Displays

- Visual aids *to build background knowledge*
- Political spectrum *to illustrate varying perspectives on an issue*
- Prompts *to stimulate discussions*
- Quotes by historical and contemporary figures *to inspire student actions and interactions*
- Current event articles from journals, newspapers, and magazines *to connect to students' daily lives*
- Examples of professionals in social studies–related pursuits *to identify social studies careers*
- Maps *to show political, historical, economic, physical, topographic, road, and climate information*
- Time lines *to relate the perspectives of time and events in the past or present*
- Rubrics *to show criteria for student work*
- Displays *to recognize students' accomplishments*

COLLECT MATERIALS AND RESOURCES

It is time to brainstorm the kinds of materials and resources you would like to use to make your curriculum and instruction come alive. Consider what you want to use to illustrate concepts emphasized in your units and lessons such as maps, charts, photographs, artifacts (Obenchain & Morris, 2003), and realia (Maxim, 2006). What primary source documents will you want your students to examine? What online resources will you access, such as the Library of Congress or National Archives? Look through the textbooks to identify the topics and issues to start your thoughts. Can you find these materials in a local teacher supply store? Does the school have resources? Are these items available online? Is there an educational catalog you can borrow from your school's department chair or librarian? Additionally, do you want specific items, such as magnifying glasses to look at documents, or supplies, such as graph paper or construction paper, for the students to use in class?

It is also wise to begin collecting materials to help you get organized, such as plastic crates, stackable baskets, or colored file folders. You will keep some of these items in your classroom, some in the department or grade level office, and some at home. You will be amazed how quickly supplemental materials will accumulate, and in social studies, they take up a great amount of room.

ESTABLISH YOUR POLICIES AND PROCEDURES

There are three sources to consult as you establish your classroom policies and procedures. You will need to comply with regulations adopted by the school district (i.e., dress code and weapons), school building (i.e., hall passes and tardies), and your team or department (i.e., interactions and assignments). You want to be firm, fair, consistent, and, most of all, patient as you reflect all three layers of regulations and express your own style. Keep in mind that, for most of you, your students spend only one class session a day with you. They move through many different spaces and try to comply with everyone's expectations. You want to create an environment that communicates your plans and makes teaching and learning the focus of the school day.

> *The teacher takes a paper and asks students to tell a rule, and writes [it] down if that is [a] good [one] then passes the paper around and has students write their names.*

> Anusha, age 9, Grade 4

You have several choices in establishing classroom policies and procedures. Although you could simply tell your students how you expect them to act in your classroom, we encourage you to model effective social studies by brainstorming possibilities, examining rationale, and reaching consensus. Try accomplishing this during the first few days of class. Divide the class into small cooperative learning groups, and ask each group to construct a list of classroom expectations along with associated consequences (rewards and punishments). Prompt your students to write the list as positive rather than negative statements. You will have to decide if you want to call them rules or if that term conveys negativity.

You might be amazed at the detailed lists your students will generate. Through consensus, you and your students can determine which expectations to adopt and how they will be managed. You will discover that some items can be grouped together into one overarching expectation, some items have multiple implications, and some items you need to maintain control. These discoveries are all part of the negotiation and consensus building—excellent models of social studies processes used in the real world. If you have multiple classes, you will have to decide if you want one set of expectations for all your classes or if you want to customize the expectations for each of your classes. Keep in mind the need to revisit and revise both the expectations and the processes from time to time, just as citizens revisit and revise governmental and business regulations.

> *Teachers need to collaborate with students, but know basically what they want.*

> Ann, age 14, Grade 9

When you talk with your colleagues, you may find that most of them follow similar procedures. This approach makes it much easier for your students and for you. If you like the procedures, we suggest that you try something similar. Then you can discuss the outcome with your team to make changes as a group or individually.

CREATE A SHARED LEARNING ENVIRONMENT

Your goal is to make your classroom a shared learning environment. Therefore, you need to refer to it as "our classroom" rather than "my classroom." The same advice applies to your classroom management. By setting expectations together, you and your students share a sense of ownership and responsibility relative to how everyone will participate in the shared learning community.

From one experienced teacher: "*Since this is a social studies class, I use charts similar to the United States' branches of government and how a bill becomes a law to communicate my system of classroom management. The first chart shows three boxes: expectations of the school, expectations of the teacher, and expectations of the students. Each box has a few items listed; together we list a few more items. The second chart shows a flowchart of rewards and consequences. I complete most of the charts in advance, but together we finish the charts. I repeat this exercise with each class during the first day. Then I consolidate all of the charts into one final version. In this way, I start the first day by doing social studies.*"

Some student expectations from the school and/or district include:

1. Wear clothing in compliance with the dress code.

2. Respect all people and the school campus.

3. Avoid gum, tobacco products, cell phones, and music players on campus.

Some student expectations from the teachers include:

1. Arrive to class on time ready to participate.

2. Bring supplies and assignments to class everyday.

3. Do your best on every assignment.

Some student expectations from the students include:

1. Talk only at appropriate times and in consideration of other speakers.

2. Use polite language and speaking tones.

3. Take responsibility for your actions.

HOLD CLASS MEETINGS REGULARLY

One way to build community is to hold class meetings (Marzano, Marzano, & Pickering, 2003). After all, an effective class meeting is social studies in action right there in your classroom. Let your students know when class meetings will be held, such as every other Monday, and how long they will last, such as fifteen minutes. You will not need to dedicate an entire class session to a class meeting unless you have a large agenda, such as an upcoming school event or a growing classroom dilemma. You can lead the meeting or, after time and modeling, your students can lead the meeting. The goal is to create a shared learning environment.

Construct an agenda and post the agenda, just as you expect your school administrators and public officials to do for and with you. Invite your students to submit agenda items by a stipulated deadline, such as one day before the meeting. Your students will be quite impressed that they have a genuine voice. As you guide your students through the first few meetings, explain each step to them and remind them that, although this is a shared experience, you are the teacher and will make the final decisions on which items you will discuss, the order, and the amount of time spent on each. You must maintain this responsibility. Some of your students may take advantage of a class meeting and suggest agenda items that are uncomfortable or inappropriate. They also may want to extend the length of the classroom meeting to avoid doing other work.

During the class meeting, follow the agenda and ask a student to serve as scribe to record the notes. You can select a scribe using name cards or sticks. Again, you will have to model your expectations explicitly. Using large chart paper, the overhead projector, or an ELMO (electric light machine operation) is effective and you have a copy of the notes to keep.

Preview the entire agenda and state the approximate length of time you plan to dedicate to each item. Doing this helps students manage their energies too. They know that you expect to discuss an issue and determine an outcome rather quickly, or that you plan to introduce an item that will take several class meetings to decide the most appropriate action. Give each student the opportunity to speak during the meeting, and hold the meetings when all students are present.

Once you have conducted the first few class meetings, your students will start contributing more agenda items and begin realizing that they have both voice and choice. For these outcomes to happen, you must conduct an authentic class meeting and follow through on the class decisions.

ENSURE EQUITY AND FAIRNESS

You want to be fair (Danielson, 1996), you want your students to understand fairness and act fairly, you want to ensure fairness among your students, and you want your students to appreciate fairness in the classroom and in the world. Fairness entails a significant concept of social studies that assures everyone is provided equity and justice. Think of this as providing everyone equal information, access, and opportunity (Gallavan, in press) for effective learning and living.

Equity and fairness do not mean you treat all students the very same. Some students will require more time and attention; some students will need less energy. You need to be aware of each of your student's individual needs and interests so you can provide for them appropriately. And not all students will need the same amount of time and attention at the same time. Equity and fairness should be considered in terms of what you think or believe is a student's past performance, a student's immediate progress, and what you predict is a student's long-term potential. These conditions are all important aspects of equity and fairness. The triad of performance, progress, and potential can guide you in working with your students throughout the school year. (See Box 1.3)

USE APPROPRIATE
AND NEUTRAL LANGUAGE

Your students and their families look to you as a positive role model. For some of your students, you are one of the few educated individuals who can help prepare them for their future studies and career success. And for some of your students, English is a new language. They need to hear and see proper English in both formal and informal conversations and written communications.

Using gender-neutral language is important for both modeling and inclusion. Be aware of your word choices so your female

Box 1.3   Suggestions for Establishing Equity and Fairness

1. Establish and maintain high academic and social expectations for all of your students at all times.
2. Share expectations with students and parents in writing.
3. Model and reinforce respect and politeness with everyone at all times.
4. Apologize sincerely when you make a mistake.
5. Provide specific feedback and show genuine appreciation. If you applaud for one presentation, the goal is to applaud for all.
6. Allow students to finish speaking and redirect interruptions, although you may have to ask students to keep their comments to a limited amount of time.
7. Select students equitably using name cards, sticks, or tokens (for questions, comments, activities, errands, and so forth). All students need to know that they should be prepared at all times and that you have both the right and responsibility to call on them at any time.
8. Delve fairly; this means that you probe and follow up with all students using higher-order and critical thinking.
9. Use a stopwatch or clock to monitor ample wait time when asking students questions to answer or giving them instructions to demonstrate an action. Your students will appreciate the consistency.
10. Establish clear consequences for students who cannot show respect and fairness for others.

students feel valued and all your students experience the power of language. When addressing your students collectively, call them ladies and gentlemen rather than girls and boys or guys for everyone. When referencing professions use words such as firefighter and police officer rather than fireman and policeman. Use the term *humankind*, rather than *mankind*, when talking about all people. You might want to ask a colleague to listen to your word choices to be sure you are using appropriate and gender-neutral language.

The same guidelines apply to using culturally sensitive language. You want to be aware if you use any inappropriate cultural references or imply bias. Sometimes teachers make comments that communicate prejudice such as referring to all houses of worship as churches that are attended on or only on Sundays, people without jobs as irresponsible or poor, and so forth. All educators must be cognizant of their word choices. And, particularly as social studies teachers, we should lead others in this effort.

KNOW YOUR LEARNERS

With the diversity of today's society, you will likely have students representing different heritages, different customs, different countries, and different languages. They bring a variety of past school experiences with them along with different learning abilities, some more successful than others. You will need to get to know your students on an individual basis.

> *Social studies teachers show they care about you by taking an interest in you. They will acknowledge you if you are doing well, and help you if you aren't doing well. They might also ask about things going on in your life.*
>
> Amy, age 13, Grade 8

The relationships you establish with your students will motivate them to achieve and to continue to achieve (Tomlinson & McTighe, 2006). When students perceive that teachers care about them and their levels of achievement, they will be more likely to engage in the classroom. Take time to get to know your students. Use surveys and interest inventories, talk to them individually and in small groups, use dialogue journals, solicit their opinions, have them share their perspectives. For example, many teachers have students mark a place on a laminated map indicating where they were born or where they have lived or traveled. They ask students to write autobiographies and share special talents or hobbies. Social studies classes provide great opportunities for social interactions.

> *Teachers can show they care for you by remembering the little things. Such as when your birthday is, or that you like dogs. Another way is by asking how your weekend was, and then actually listening to the answer.*
>
> Linda, age 15, Grade 10

Feedback from students is the most compelling evidence and provides clear guidelines for teachers. In prioritizing their comments about teachers, social studies students say they want teachers who like their students and care about them as individuals; control the class so that students have a chance to learn what they need and want to learn; demonstrate fairness in their classroom interactions, assignments and assessments; know how to teach and help students succeed; and know their content and make it interesting (Gallavan, in press).

> *Help students with everything you can. You should also never give up on them no matter how their grades are.*

> Trevor, age 15, Grade 10

REALIZE CHANGES IN TODAY'S STUDENTS

One of the most important points when reflecting on your teaching entails the changes in today's students. Keep in mind that you are no longer the student, you are no longer the age of your students, and that today's students are different from you (Wallis & Steptoe, 2006).

Today's students can think broadly and holistically, yet they prefer to concentrate on minutiae. They can operate in an interdisciplinary manner in both form and function while focused on a single event, but they are more concrete than abstract thinkers. They approach problem solving and decision making eagerly as a personal challenge utilizing resources and creating solutions. They like the responsibility and productivity of their own advancement; however, some of today's students exhibit limited attention span and perseverance.

Many of today's students are smarter and more comfortable with current technology than you are now. They embrace technology as a way of thinking, acting, and communicating. Some say today's students are technology natives since they grew up with much of the technology we take for granted today. Today's students can be a bit impatient if and when technology is unavailable or fails to operate as expected.

Today's students like to work cooperatively and in teams. They like the group spirit and a feeling of helping others succeed . . . as long they also succeed individually. They think of themselves as rather special; they have been overly organized and extremely sheltered (Howe & Strauss, 2000). Many of them have been involved in all kinds of team sports and been given all kinds of awards. However, today's students tend to be extremely competitive, feel pressured to produce and achieve, and see winning as a way to be financially comfortable. Schools have gravitated away from cooperative learning and teamwork thereby placing today's students at a disadvantage. Social studies can help develop these skills.

Today's students may know more about the world than you knew when you were their age, or maybe more than you know now. (Some of them know that information is power and like having that power.) Many more of them seem to know isolated pieces of information and need help connecting the dots. They may not always see the world on a global scale and the interplay among nations, governments, and economies.

You must stay ahead of your students, and you must view the world from multiple perspectives. In general, today's students value diversity and avoid prejudice, bias, and stereotyping. Many of today's students are or have multiracial and multilingual family members, divide their lives with many different family members, and practice many different faiths and beliefs.

INVOLVE PARENTS AND FAMILIES

> *I liked that by doing our family tree we were learning about our ancestors and where they came from along with their names.*

> Vanessa, age 9, Grade 4

You have many different avenues for inviting your students' parents into your classroom. They are a wonderful resource and the more you include them, the more effective you will be as a teacher. Parents and family members will understand your purposes and situation more clearly when they visit; they are more likely to listen and support you if you encounter difficulties with their children; and they will contribute their expertise to your classroom.

From a new teacher: "*Once a week I make a plan to contact at least three parents for what I like to call 'Community Connection.' These are always positive calls. I find out students' interests and family ties and give updates on student progress.*"

You can ask for parent volunteers to either work with you in the classroom and with individual students and/or to assist you with clerical work and special events. Talk with your department chair and colleagues to investigate how other teachers involve parents. If you want parents in your classroom, think carefully about their roles and their interactions with students. This would be a great topic to discuss at a classroom meeting with your students too.

Another way to involve parents and family members in your classroom is to invite them to discuss their professions, travels, hobbies, special interests, personal life experiences, and so forth. Send home a survey at the beginning of the school year with specific topics and issues to solicit potential speakers. You may discover that your students' parents have much to share on topics relevant to your curriculum. We give you more guidelines about doing this in Chapter 9.

A veteran teacher tells us, "*My most successful assignments were those that involved parents and students' own likes. I had parents come in and share their '60s' experiences by just telling the students what life was like growing up during that decade.*"

Your school will sponsor all kinds of special events related to social studies such as holiday festivals, unit culminations, geography bees, history day competitions, career days, and so forth. You will want to invite parents and family members to participate in many different capacities. You might need help with food, decorations, sales, judging, score keeping, prizes, and so forth. These are ideal opportunities to connect with parents, strengthen relationships with students, and extend your classroom. We provide you with more ideas in Chapter 11.

Also, we recommend that you look at *Secrets to Success for Beginning Elementary Teachers* (2007) or *Secrets for Secondary School Teachers: How to Succeed in Your First Year* (2004) by Corwin Press for specific suggestions on organizing your room and creating communities of learners.

BEGIN EACH DAY ANEW

Be ready for each class and greet students every day. This means having all of your teaching materials arranged in advance. Find a spot where you will stand and welcome students as they enter the classroom. This may be the same spot where you stand after you close the learning as you dismiss the students. Following these routines will let your students know you are approachable and help you stay organized.

Include a moment at the beginning of each class for everyone to get settled. This is the perfect time for you to share some current events and help your students take a breath to focus on social studies before you launch into your agenda. The more you can model and reinforce a positive and productive manner, the more your students will participate and achieve.

Establish a Sense of Place . . .

You've dreamed of this day, and now it is here. You want this classroom to be an inviting, exciting, and rewarding space where everyone engages in and contributes to the learning experience. The secret is creating a safe and welcoming sense of place. Help the students feel comfortable around you and with social studies. When students walk in the door, they will immediately experience that this is a social studies classroom. Now you are ready to think about your curriculum.

Suggested Activities

1. Design your ideal classroom. Consider the following:
   - Placement and movement
   - Information and displays
   - Resources and references
   - Materials and supplies
   - Presentations and demonstrations
   - Equipment and storage

2. Develop one display, preferably interactive, that will attract your students' attention and motivate their interests in a captivating social studies topic or issue.

3. Brainstorm and share ways to connect social studies concepts to the contemporary world of your students throughout the week. These may include pictures of students' activities and articles of interest to them.

4. On a bulletin board, feature a small group of students in each class each week. Construct a list of items that students can display including photographs, accomplishments, travels, interests, and so forth.

CHAPTER TWO

Understand Standards *to Develop Your Curriculum*

L et's review what social studies is, does, and involves. It is important that we establish a common foundation as we proceed through this book. All of us appreciate having a description of social studies available at our fingertips for clarifying our purposes and communicating our work with our students, their parents, and other educators.

APPRECIATE THE BENEFITS OF SOCIAL STUDIES

Social studies encompasses the philosophies, forms, and functions that enable us to understand the world holistically (Gallavan, 2003). Social studies allows us to easily comprehend the past, equips us to successfully perform in the present, and prepares us to readily process new information and predict the future from multiple viewpoints.

The acquiring of social studies knowledge, skills, and attitudes or dispositions[1] helps us to achieve academically as students and to operate successfully as citizens living in an interdependent, global society. From social studies, we learn how to read and make maps, how to select and develop careers, how to invest our money and balance our checkbooks, how to understand politics and vote, how to become active and responsible members of our communities, and so forth. As you can see, we benefit greatly from the breadth and depth of school experiences that introduce and explore social studies through a diverse assortment of avenues and interactions that actively engage and respectfully challenge us.

RECOGNIZE THE NATURE OF SOCIAL STUDIES

Social studies involves the examination of humans—our thoughts, beliefs, languages, experiences, actions, and certainly, our interactions—locally to globally. Yet, social studies is not a pre-scribed list of static or isolated facts, figures, times, places, and people to be memorized and recited upon request. No such list could be identified, managed, or agreed on easily by our diverse U.S. society, a citizenry firmly founded on its freedoms regulating individual thought, speech, and actions.

Realizing that social studies entails comprehending an abun-dance of information, accessing limitless resources, experiencing various opportunities, and seeing the world from diverse points of view, we must recognize that the nature of social studies strongly depends on its sociocultural context (Vygotsky, 1978; Wink, 2004) or the situation and circumstances in which it is studied. This means that social studies needs to be relevant to the current and immediate time, space, participants, events, norms, and values. Simply put, social studies is about us—all of us, here and now.

DIG INTO THE HISTORY OF SOCIAL STUDIES EDUCATION

When the United States was founded, educated citizens studied mainly history, geography, and government among the other tra-ditional subjects, such as literature and the arts. The curriculum did not include social studies until the early twentieth century. During the second half of the nineteenth century, U.S. citizens began redefining themselves as a nation, while similar efforts occurred within the country's educational systems. The emergence of urbanization, immigration, industrialization, and the middle class (Lybarger in Shaver, 1991) now influenced the concerns of five special interest groups regarding the role of social studies in the new school reform movement (Kliebard, 1986). Social studies curriculum, content, and control were targeted by: humanists, social efficiency educators, child development educators, social reconstructionist educators, and life adjustment educators. As you can surmise, these groups did not agree on the purposes of social studies. Fortunately, none of these groups dominated nor should have dominated the teaching of social studies. (See Box 2.1)

Box 2.1   Special Interest Groups in New School Reform

- Humanists—Individuals who want to equip students with important knowledge fundamental to the lifelong human experience

- Social Efficiency Educators—Individuals who design new curricular content to prepare students for their future roles and responsibilities of adulthood

- Child Development Educators—Individuals who aim to align curriculum with students' ages and developmental levels to meet their natural needs and interests

- Social Reconstructionist Educators—Individuals who hope to use curricular content to combat social injustices and to promote institutional societal change through social reform

- Life Adjustment Educators—Individuals who combine selected efforts of social efficiency, child development, and reconstructionist education

SOURCE: Adapted from Kliebard (1986).

EXAMINE THE PURPOSES
OF SOCIAL STUDIES

In 1916, a report was written by the National Education Association Committee on Social Studies for the Reorganization of Secondary Education establishing social studies as a vital field of study important to U.S. students, schooling, and society (Lybarger in Shaver, 1991). This early committee recommended that social studies focus on vocational and community civics, American democracy, European and American history, and an interdisciplinary approach collectively referencing civics, economics, geography, history, psychology, and sociology (Tyrone, 1934). Early social studies was built on these foundations to achieve three purposes:

- Transmission of citizenship education
- Knowledge of the social science
- Comprehension of reflective inquiry (Barr, Barth, & Shermis, 1978)

Five years later, in 1921, the National Council for the Social Studies (NCSS) was organized to help inform, guide, and support the field of social studies in prekindergarten through the twelfth grades (Lybarger in Shaver, 1991). Their initial mission focused on expanding the curriculum; many educators felt that learning history alone was not an adequate preparation for citizenship in an increasingly complex global society.

KNOW THE NCSS DEFINITION

NCSS (1994, p. 3) offers this definition: "Social studies is the integrated study of the social sciences and humanities to promote civic competence. Within the school program, social studies provides coordinated, systematic study drawing upon such disciplines as anthropology/archeology, economics, geography, history, law/ethics, philosophy, political science, psychology, religion, and sociology, as well as appropriate content from the humanities, mathematics, and natural science."

This definition is a compilation of the academic researched disciplines, the curricular content areas, and the pedagogical and programmatic approaches necessary for the teaching and learning of social studies found in the secondary social studies classrooms. This all-encompassing definition successfully guides and supports middle level, middle school, and junior high school teachers, as well as high school teachers with respect to course content and classroom configuration. Focusing on the holistic outcome of civic competence, NCSS allows and encourages social studies teachers to create their own learning environments to achieve their goals.

RELY ON THE NCSS CURRICULAR STRANDS

In 1994, the NCSS published *Expectations of Excellence* (NCSS, 1994) providing educators with this operating definition. The book also identifies ten thematically based curricular strands with corresponding sets of performance expectations and illustrations of exemplary teaching and learning selected to accompany each of the ten strands. They are: Culture; Time, Continuity, and Change; People, Places, and Environments; Individual Development and Identity; Individuals, Groups, and Institutions; Power, Authority, and Governance; Production, Distribution, and Consumption; Science, Technology, and Society; Global Connections; and Civic Ideals and Practices. Note the strands you will you address in your classes.

DEVELOP PRACTICAL APPLICATIONS OF EACH STRAND

To see what social studies would look like in a classroom setting, the ten thematic strands with descriptions and practical examples of student activities applicable to various subject areas are described as follows:

   I. **Culture**—The innate, learned, and shared characteristics describing one's self-identity as an individual and as a member of various groups in ways that are similar to and different from other individuals and group members; static and dynamic qualities associated with our diverse thoughts, beliefs, language, actions, interactions, values, traditions, customs, and expectations

Examples:

A. Bring an artifact from home to describe the importance of realia and symbols in your personal life as expressions of our family heritage and cultural characteristics.

B. Create a graphic organizer noting some of the more common symbols found among various world cultures.

II. Time, Continuity, and Change—Connections with the past, present, and future through our own experiences and memories as well as the events and stories of others; various and frequently conflicting histories and perspectives that allow us to understand our history, seeing how things stay the same and how they differ over time

Examples:

A. Draw a time line showing significant events, discoveries, and changes in your own life.

B. Collect an oral history from a family member or friend to delve into a story related to your family or neighborhood and the changes over time.

III. People, Places, and Environments—The physical and human geographic characteristics and interactions seen from multiple viewpoints; the relationships between nature and humans with implications for the world around us near and far

Examples:

A. Draw and label a map of your favorite room or space in or around your home.

B. Reference various maps to probe a local issue or common concern related to the use of land, water, and/or air.

IV. Individual Development and Identity—The characteristics, growth, and changes made by an individual as a member of various groups in a variety of environments and situations; the thoughts, beliefs, languages, actions, and interactions used by an individual to process and express one's understanding of people, places, and events

Examples:

A. Craft several goals (academic, social, emotional, physical) and design specific steps to achieve those goals; maintain a running record of progress.

B. Read a biography about an individual with whom you identify; write and share three qualities that you want to acquire.

V. Individuals, Groups, and Institutions—The integral roles played by individuals, groups, institutions, and/or organizations and their relationships in our society; the influences and impacts that various individuals, groups, and/or institutions enact upon communities, states, and the nation

Examples:

A. List three personal characteristics that make you unique and special.

B. Describe an institution in the immediate community and contributions the institution makes.

VI. Power, Authority, and Governance—The functions and contributions of individuals, groups, and organizations in making decisions and exhibiting leadership; the formal and informal relationships among roles, rights, rules, responsibilities, and respect

Examples:

A. Design a chart showing leadership traits that are more and less effective.

B. Invite a guest speaker from city government or a private business to describe steps for successful decision making.

VII. Production, Distribution, and Consumption—The availability of natural and human-made resources; the interdependent, decision making that impacts their roles in our lives

Examples:

A. Name one product and one service of importance to you; explain how they are related to each other and why they are important to you.

B. Trace a popular cooking recipe to its roots around the world.

VIII. Science, Technology, and Society—The explorations, discoveries, and inventions over time; their influences and impacts on individuals, groups, institutions, and organizations

Examples:

A. Describe how technology has improved the quality of your life and what technology you would like to see made a part of our everyday lives.

B. Identify three inventions that are no longer in use today and tell what newer inventions have replaced them.

IX. Global Connections—The interrelationships among people from around the world; the influences and impacts that individuals, groups, and institutions enact upon one another from the past, through the present, and into the future

Examples:

A. Name one place outside of the country that you would like to visit and tell why you would like to visit there.

B. Identify an issue of global concern and show how various outcomes will affect various countries or parts of the planet.

X. Civic Ideals and Practices—The beliefs and actions related to democratic principles, social justice, and participatory citizenship; the roles, rights, and responsibilities of the peoples within a society

Examples:

A. Help organize and conduct a school election; run for office.

B. Study the human rights of children around the world and the advantages for children living in the United States.

The ten strands often seem like remote, abstract ideas to students, particularly younger learners. The secret is to help them identify concrete examples and make personal connections. Effective teachers guide students in making comparisons to what they are studying with their own lives.

A veteran teacher notes: *"Aid students in seeing that people are people. People from hundreds of years ago are a lot like some people today. Make a continuous correlation between the life being discussed and someone with whom the students can relate. Recently we were discussing Rasputin and how he died of drowning after being poisoned, shot twice, and beaten. Students remarked that Rasputin reminded them of the rapper, 50 Cent, who has also defied assassination attempts."*

DRAW FROM THE ACADEMIC DISCIPLINES

We cannot begin a discussion of social studies standards without recognizing all of the academic disciplines contributing to this interdisciplinary field of study. We like to think of social studies beginning as a river and the contributing disciplines as the streams that flow into the river. The river grows deeper and stronger as more streams and rivers—the contributions of the arts, humanities, and integrated curriculum—enter. Social studies becomes the ocean, and the ocean is three-fourths of the planet Earth. Staying with this analysis, we encourage you to consider social studies as the context that holds all of the other subject areas together. And like water, social studies gives the other subject areas life.

The ten main academic disciplines and their primary processes are identified and described as follows:

1. *Anthropology/Archeology*—Identifies individual and shared backgrounds, heritages, and relationships over time and through space; values the rich diversity of cultural characteristics relevant for understanding who we are and how we interact

2. *Economics*—Analyzes the production, distribution, exchange, and consumption of productive resources (natural, human, capital goods, and services) to supply wants and needs; develops an understanding of opportunity and cost with sound economic policy connected with real life and the world of work

3. *Geography*—Makes sense of the world's physical and human attributes and divisions; understands and integrates the five themes of geography including location, sense of place, relationships between humans and environments, movement, and regions inclusive of contemporary geopolitical concerns and conversations

4. *History*—Views persons, places, and events from the ancient to the immediate past as contributing significantly to our contemporary existence while establishing the foundations of the future; pursues the content, processes, and context that help us to understand and appreciate the historical themes encapsulated in patterns and forces among social, political, economic, and religious interactions

5. *Law/Ethics*—Delves into the concepts and practices ensuring democratic principles and social justice equitably; links legal issues and moral dilemmas in society by modeling inquiries in schools and classrooms through active involvement, community construct, conflict resolution, and application to life and literature

6. *Philosophy*—Deliberates the breadth, depth, and diversity of ideas informing all of the social sciences throughout time, the ways in which ideas influence action and interaction, and the changes we experience individually and as a society

7. *Political Science*—Probes the concepts of order and reason accompanied with the complexity of issues and multiple perspectives impacting the principles, organizations, and methods of government; studies systems of governance, power, authority, and responsibility as vital aspects of change over time

8. *Psychology*—Considers the ways and reasons people think, believe, and act as individuals, among other individuals, and within organizations; reflects deeply while analyzing logically and purposefully one's motivations, behaviors, and reinforcements, within the ever-changing characteristics of multidimensional relationships

9. *Religion*—Contemplates the principles and practices that individuals and groups select and honor to distinguish and guide their lives and the importance that different societies place upon various religious influences; researches religion objectively by neither promoting nor demoting any particular belief or behavior

10. *Sociology*—Investigates how individuals operate as interdependent members of various groups; explores how individuals and groups act and interact to achieve common purposes; experiences grouping as members of families and communities and as intricate parts of a diverse, international, global society

At times, your teaching may emphasize primarily one discipline, yet you will draw from each throughout the year. We think this approach will appeal to your students. All of you will include current events in some way. Perhaps you want your students to become more aware of the world around them in general, or perhaps a specific event has occurred that you want to bring to your students' attention.

For example, if you are teaching citizenship or government, current events reflect contemporary trends, particularly trends demonstrated by young people. If you are teaching economics, current events reveal local, national, and global market patterns. If you are teaching geography, current events are useful to show weather and natural disasters. If you are teaching history, current events show change over time. As you can see, current events also involve anthropology and culture; law, ethics, and criminology at all levels; and aspects of philosophy, psychology, religion, political science, and sociology. You could easily use any current event to connect all ten academic disciplines of social studies to the interests of your students.

The social sciences are not limited to the ten academic disciplines. The social sciences also include: architecture, career education, conflict management resolution skills, environmental education, global education, health education, international education, life skills, multicultural education, and urban education. Content and practices from each of these social studies are evident in many middle level and high school social studies courses.

Identify the disciplines for which you will be primarily responsible. As of this writing we are aware of the following nationally developed voluntary standards in specific disciplines:

- *National Content Standards for Economics*—National Council on Economic Education
- *National Geography Standards*—National Council for Geographic Education
- *National Standards for Civics and Government*—Center for Civic Education
- *National Standards for History, Basic Edition*—National Center for History in the Schools
- *Voluntary National Content Standards in Economics*—National Council on Economic Education
- *National Standards for the Teaching of High School Psychology*—American Psychological Association

NOTE THE NCSS
PURPOSE, VISION, AND APPROACHES

"The primary purpose of social studies is to help young people develop their abilities to make informed and reasoned decisions for the public good as citizens of a culturally diverse, democratic society in an interdependent world" (NCSS, 1994, p. 3). Ultimately, the NCSS goal is for students to be ready to assume, as Thomas Jefferson called it, the "office of citizen" (NCSS, 1994, p. 3).

The NCSS vision states that social studies should "help students develop social understanding and civic efficacy" (NCSS, 1994, p. 3). Although teachers in the field of social studies do not always agree on the best content nor the preferred way(s) for accomplishing this vision (Lybarger in Shaver, 1991), a combined list of beliefs identifies six traditional approaches toward social studies education that have arisen since its inception in 1916 (Brophy & Alleman, 1996; Martorella, 1994).

The six traditional approaches encompass the study of:

1. *Social Sciences*—by relying on specific disciplinary knowledge and scholarly research related to the discrete academic fields of study;

2. *Citizenship Transmission*—by teaching traditional knowledge, skills, dispositions, and values as the accepted framework for understanding self, others, and society and for making decisions;

3. *Reflective Inquiry*—by thinking critically, asking questions, researching conditions, analyzing values, and making decisions regarding social policy and civic issues within the ever-changing nature of knowledge, contributing to resolving issues significant to humanity;

4. *Cultural Heritage*—by examining and celebrating the roles of and contributions from all citizens within our local and global societies relevant to the past, present, and future;

5. *Social Criticism*—by providing students with informed and authentic experiential learning opportunities to examine, discover, construct, critique, and revise past traditions, existing social practices, and accepted modes of debate and analysis in application to the contemporary concern and social policy issues; and

6. *Personal Development*—by developing a positive self-concept and a strong sense of persona or self-efficacy.

Ironically, the six traditional approaches tend to simultaneously complement and compete with one another. Although most social studies teachers tend to ascribe to only one or two of these social sciences approaches, they know they need to incorporate all six approaches and give the learning purpose in an integrated holistic manner.

For example, if you are teaching a unit of learning on immigration to the United States and the changing demographics over time, you could approach this topic from any or all six of the approaches as shown in Table 2.1.

Table 2.1   Six Traditional Social Studies Approaches to Teaching U.S. Immigration

Approach	*Example*
1. Social Sciences	Identify how many people came from each country and the dates of their immigration
2. Citizenship Transmission	Discuss various concerns that immigrants encounter in traveling to and entering the U.S. as well as the various reactions of the U.S. citizens
3. Reflective Inquiry	Investigate how immigration has changed over time and the impacts on the United States
4. Cultural Heritage	Share the contributions of various immigrants, the creation of U.S. heritage, and the continual changes over time
5. Social Criticism	Look at current issues relevant to immigration and their impacts on U.S. government, laws, and economics from multiple, conflicting, perspectives
6. Personal Development	Research one's own immigration to the United States and exchange stories with other students to appreciate the rich and diverse history of the United States

SOURCE: Adapted from Brophy and Alleman (1996) and Martorella (1994).

REFERENCE YOUR STATE STANDARDS

States have written social studies standards or academic frameworks that can be found on their state department of education Web sites. They are frequently based on NCSS standards and the voluntary national standards. It is vital that you know how to locate the standards and have a copy of these documents at your fingertips when developing your curriculum and planning your lessons. Many school administrations require their teachers to note the specific state standard(s) they are teaching in their written plans they turn in to their administrators weekly and to post them daily for all to see.

A veteran teacher explains: *"We always begin our session by looking at the state standard we are going to cover that day. We note our progress as the year goes on."*

In many states, the standards or frameworks also are presented by grade level and/or course syllabi. You can go directly to a specific grade level or course where you will find many of the following:

- Essential understandings, that is the big ideas, such as why we have laws, supported by specific knowledge and skills
- Learning expectations or objectives
- Grade-level benchmarks
- Aligned assessments
- Teaching strategies for each standard

In addition, many state documents include glossaries, sample learning scenarios, ideas for cross-curricular integration, and Internet references.

These resources provide you with a solid foundation necessary for constructing your own curriculum.

While state standards for social studies are numerous, states and/or districts may prioritize the standards for teachers formally. For example, one state we know categorized the standards as *Worth Being Familiar With, Important to Know,* or *Enduring Understanding* based on the work of Wiggins and McTighe (2006). In other places, teachers work together to distinguish "power" standards: the ones they feel are most essential from those that are "nice to know" and those that will best prepare students for the next level of work based on the work of Ainsworth (2003).

As one teacher says: *"You have to pick and choose what you have time for, combining standards where possible. You cannot cover everything in the textbook."*

INCORPORATE YOUR DISTRICT EXPECTATIONS

You also need to be well acquainted with your school district's academic expectations. Most likely you will be given a copy (print or digital) of the district's Scope and Sequence Guide or told where to find it on the Web. This guide allows you to see what courses are taught at each grade level along with what is expected of your particular grade level and courses (scope) within the context of other grade levels and courses (sequence). A typical sequence can be found in Table 2.2.

School district expectations are built upon state standards or frameworks. Some school districts have identified topics, issues, sample lesson plans, and suggested forms of assessment with rubrics for each grade level and course syllabi. These resources were created to enhance your effectiveness and success based on state expectations and the students in your district. The secret is they will also help you pace your instruction.

Keep in mind that all students need to have mastered all of the knowledge and skills for the previous grade levels regardless of what is expected at their current grade level. That means that teachers and students in Grade 10 are responsible for all standards in Grades K–9 in addition to the standards for Grade 10. We would like to think that all of the previous standards have been taught and learned. Yet, teachers understand that their students come with varying learning experiences and achievement levels and they benefit from revisiting the standards set for earlier grades throughout the school year.

FEATURE YOUR SCHOOL ORGANIZATION AND MISSION

Finally, it is important to look at your school's organization and mission. Some schools are neighborhood schools, some are magnet schools, some are technical or vocational, and others are partners with community colleges. Some schools are divided into houses or

Table 2.2   Typical Social Studies Scope and Sequence

Grade Level	Social Studies Course
5th	Interdisciplinary social studies; U.S. geography and history
6th	Interdisciplinary social studies; world geography and history
7th	State social studies (economics, geography, government, and history)
8th	One semester of world geography, one semester of economics, or two semesters of U.S. history
9th	Civics/citizenship/government
10th	World history

11th	U.S. history
	Optional electives (one or two semesters):
	    Sociology
	    Psychology
	    Anthropology

12th	U.S. government
	U.S. government (one semester); economics (one semester)
	Optional electives (one or two semesters):
	    Sociology
	    Psychology
	    Anthropology

academies. Your school may have a special emphasis, such as languages and culture, environmental education, international relations, and so forth. Your school may host a particular event or participate in a special competition annually that is a part of the social studies. We know of one school that requires all of its seventh-graders to complete a History Day project. Another school involves all of its students in fourth through eighth grades in the National Geographic Bee. These events are part of the school's organization and culture.

Usually you can find the school's mission statement published in the school handbook, posted on the school Web site, and/or displayed in the school entranceway. Many schools have crafted mission statements that sound something like this: "At our school, we are a community formed of students, families, faculty, and staff committed to developing responsibility, building self-confidence, fostering lifelong learning, and providing essential experiences for daily success."

Find your school's mission statement and post it on your wall. This is an important school document to highlight in your classroom and with your students. Mission statements reflect social studies completely. Refer to your school's organization and mission statement as a way to connect your classroom, your students, and the school.

LINK REFERENCES TO DEVELOP CURRICULUM

Now that you have a clear definition of social studies and are increasing your awareness of the purposes of social studies with their supporting concepts, you can start developing your curriculum or what you are going to teach. You will rely on many different sources, including the national, state, and school district standards and expectations. You will reflect on and apply your own prior experiences as a social studies student and teacher candidate during your teacher education program. Then you can delve into the current curriculum in place at your school and collaborate with your colleagues. Table 2.3—Sample of Curriculum Planning—provides an example of how curriculum planning relies on all these references.

PLAN YOUR YEAR

We suggest that you construct a basic blueprint for the entire school year at the beginning of the school year. Take a calendar and divide sections into grading periods. Next, block out vacation days and staff development days. Note the school events, such as Open House, Back to School Night, Parent Conferences, and Homecoming. Also, indicate your district or school assessment dates (benchmark tests, if any, as well as standardized testing) on your calendar. Then, using your district curriculum guide, determine the number of units you will need to cover. Estimate the length of time for each unit, and space

Table 2.3   Sample of Curriculum Planning

Social Studies Reference	Example: Geography
Grade Level/Subject	8th Grade/World Geography
NCSS Standard	III. People, Places, and Environment
State Standard	The World in Spatial Terms: Students use maps, globes, and other geographic tools and technologies to locate, derive, and record information about people, places, and environments
School District Mission	To create and preserve an intellectually challenging and holistic learning experience that empowers learners with the knowledge, skills, and dispositions to find satisfaction as a participating member of a global society and to compete successfully in the international workplace of the future
Course Overview	Explore Earth's physical systems in a global context
Subject Standard	Construct maps and charts to display information about physical and human features
Essential Understanding or Big Idea/Topic	The planet Earth/relative size, shape, and placement of seven continents and four oceans
Learning Experience	Draw and label a map of the seven continents and four oceans from memory using paper and pencil
Integration	Literacy—Read, write, and share information about early discoverers
	Math—Measure the distance of the discoverers' routes and calculate the length of their voyages
	Science—Investigate how discoverers transported food and water and kept clean and healthy
	Arts—Examine the cartographers' details included in ancient maps

the units throughout the year. List the major topics for each unit. Though you will make changes, this guide will serve you well.

This approach will help you:

- ensure that all themes, topics, concepts, activities, and assessments are on the calendar;
- allow you to allocate and adjust the time for each unit as you want;
- help you teach in the moment and plan for the future;
- give you a plan to communicate with students, parents, and colleagues;
- satisfy a department or school accountability requirement to submit a year-long plan.

From a veteran teacher: *"It is critical to make a year-long plan to be sure everything is included at the beginning. Unfortunately, time is interrupted and I don't always get to everything, but I know it was there at the start."*

Once you have an overview, you can begin specific planning for your students. We will share a wealth of instructional practices and assessment techniques later in the book.

Connect Social Studies With Your Students . . .

Social studies is about us—all of us, here, and now. It combines our individual and collective stories. Not only do new events occur around us, simultaneously we grow, develop, and modify our understanding related to events of the past, how they influence the present, and the possibilities they offer the future. We continually adapt our thoughts, words, and actions as we socially construct and reconstruct meanings gained from both our learned and shared experiences. Teaching social studies gives you a process by which to engage all your students. The secret to success is that by identifying the social studies meaning and purpose, students will enjoy learning social studies as students and live social studies as citizens in their communities. In the next chapter we look at strategies for making instruction meaningful and empowering.

Suggested Activities

1. Reflect on your own social studies experiences. Identify one experience that helped you increase your knowledge, one experience that helped you develop your skills, and one experience that helped you expand your dispositions.

2. Find a personal artifact around your home that makes each of the ten social studies academic disciplines meaningful for you. For example, your personal meaning for anthropology might be a symbol of your heritage such as a cloverleaf if your background is Irish; your personal meaning for geography might be a map of where you were born.

3. List five current events and connect them to the academic disciplines of social studies.

4. Ask one or more of your social studies team members if you can read through their curriculum plans for a unit or the year. Note how they pace their units of instruction. See if and when benchmark assessments are given.

NOTE

1. Although the National Council for the Social Studies uses the word "attitude," we will be using the word "disposition" as it is the word most teachers and teacher educators have adopted.

CHAPTER THREE

Make Your Instruction Meaningful *to Empower Learners*

A t this point you have developed a curriculum plan or blueprint for the entire school year. You have accounted for all the dominant topics and issues identified in the state standards and academic frameworks along with the school district curricular guidelines. You have met with your colleagues and organized yourself around the grading periods and testing dates. You have checked the school calendar to include major school events so that your plan fits into your students' schedules. You have previewed the textbooks and supplementary teaching materials. Now it is time to select your instructional methods; you need to decide *how* your students are going to learn *what* you want them to learn to fulfill *why* you (and their parents) want them to learn.

BEGIN FROM THE PERSPECTIVES OF THE LEARNERS

We know you are anxious to be the teacher and start teaching; so we share this important secret to ensure your success. Select your instructional strategies from the perspectives of the learners. In other words, imagine that you are enrolled in your own class. Ask yourself some key questions that all students wonder, such as:

- Why do I have to learn this?
- What does it have to do with me?
- What do I have to do for this class?
- How much will I have to read every day?
- Will I have to (or can I) work on my own or with a partner?
- Will I make presentations in front of the class?
- Do we get to take any field trips in this class?
- Will there be any guest speakers?

These questions can help steer you as you begin to select your effective instructional strategies. You want your students to enjoy the class, to engage in their learning, and to achieve well. Reflect for a moment about your most favorite and least favorite classes. Your memories can guide you to success.

> In my sixth grade class, we were studying archaeology, so an archaeologist came in to talk to us. It was very interesting because she not only talked about what she found, but she also brought in the objects. I remember being amazed at looking at something that was over 500 years old. Also, she talked about what she did and many aspects of her job.
>
> Laura, age 14, Grade 9

SHOWCASE POWERFUL TEACHING AND LEARNING

Because your time and energy are limited, you will want to get the most out of every teachable moment. To do this, powerful teaching and learning must take place. Members of the National Council for the Social Studies (NCSS) have identified five qualities of powerful teaching and learning, stating that social studies should meet the following criteria (1994, pp. 163–170):

- *Meaningful*—Content emphasizes both how it is presented to and with students and how it is developed through activities and conversation; instruction emphasizes depth of knowledge rather than breadth of coverage, relevance of skills applicable in ever-changing environments, and quality of dispositions valuable for coping in our contemporary world. Meaningful social studies involves the sustained examination of a few topics and issues rather than superficial coverage of many different ideas and expectations.

- *Integrated*—Content includes a broad range of knowledge, skills, and dispositions that promote the six purposes of social studies centered on themes and concepts drawn from the academic disciplines of the social sciences and supplemented by the arts, sciences, and humanities. Social studies that is integrated features teaching and learning that is natural and authentic; it replicates the real world by reaching across thinking and action, people and perspectives, time and space, connection and community.

- *Value-based*—Content considers complex conditions and philosophical issues in addition to standards-based knowledge and skills. When social studies is value-based it explores differing viewpoints, ethical dimensions, potential implications, and social responsibilities. Value-based social studies encourages teachers to model and reinforce the importance of recognizing and respecting cultural diversity, conflicting opinions, and well-reasoned positions to promote human relationships.

- *Challenging*—Content encompasses knowledge, skills, and dispositions that may be new, examined from a different perspective, requires learning additional skills, or investigated as a group of learners for a different purpose. Social studies that is challenging presents new concepts or practices unlike the previously known or accepted ones; changes in concepts and practices may become controversial and contentious. Inquiry, research, conversation, and reflection are key to negotiating conflict and challenge.

- *Active*—Content engages the teacher and learner to take ownership of the learning process, guide the investigation, seek resources, make connections, and form conclusions. Social studies that is active reflects the skills necessary in life and lifelong learning in higher-order and critical thinking, problem solving, and decision making.

Each of these qualities can be easily implemented and aligned to your state content standards by the specific classroom activities you select for your students to engage in. Many examples will be presented for your consideration throughout succeeding chapters.

From a department chair: *"As I look around our classes, I see many examples of powerful teaching and learning. They include government students involved in a mock trial and economics students playing the stock market game. I've also seen geography students engaged in WebQuests throughout the year. Each of these activities allows students to 'dig deep' into a specific area of social studies."*

TEACH TO THE CORE PERFORMANCE INDICATORS

In addition, members of NCSS have written performance indicators to accompany each of the ten NCSS thematic strands (NCATE, 1997). The performance indicators specify the exact academic expectations that need to occur to fulfill each thematic strand. You should include all of the performance indicators for your social studies subject area as well as the performance indicators for related social studies subject areas. You will need to develop teaching strategies and learning experiences that are developmentally appropriate for your students.

Five of the performance indicators relate to core areas of instruction: II—Time, Continuity, and Change (history); III—People, Places, and Environments (geography); VI—Power, Authority, and Governance (civics/government/political science); VII—Production, Distribution, and Consumption (economics); and X—Civic Ideals and Practices (citizenship).

The performance indicators for thematic strands II, III, VI, VII, and X include:

II—Time, Continuity, and Change (history)
   A. Different academic explanations of events
   B. Key concepts to explain, analyze, and connect patterns
   C. Periods and patterns of change within and across cultures
   D. Processes to reconstruct and reinterpret the past
   E. Critical sensitivity for people in different contexts
   F. Decision making and action taking on public issues

III—People, Places, and Environments (geography)
   A. Mental maps
   B. Various representations of Earth
   C. Resources, tools, and cartography to generate, manipulate, and interpret information
   D. Geographic relationships
   E. Landforms and relationships in ecosystem
   F. Physical system changes and patterns that created places and reflect cultural values and ideals
   G. Physical and cultural patterns and interactions
   H. Historical events and influences on geography
   I. Social and economic effects of environmental changes
   J. Alternative uses of land and resources

VI—Power, Authority, and Governance (civics/government/political science)
   A. Persistent issues involving rights, roles, and status of individuals
   B. Purposes of government and how powers are acquired, used, and justified
   C. Governmental mechanisms to meet needs and wants of citizens
   D. National responses to forces of unity and diversity
   E. Features and leadership of the U.S. political system
   F. Conditions, actions, and motivations of conflict and cooperation within and among nations

    G. Roles of technology that contribute to and help resolve conflict

    H. Key concepts related to persistent issues and social problems

    I. Governmental attempts to achieve stated ideals at home and abroad

VII—Production, Distribution, and Consumption (economics)

    A. Choices related to goods and services, production and distribution

    B. Supply, demand, prices, incentives, and profit in a competitive market

    C. Private and public goods and services

    D. Economic system institutions

    E. Specialization and exchange

    F. Influence of values and beliefs on economic decisions

    G. Exchange and money

    H. Basic systems and who determines production, distribution, and consumption

    I. Key concepts related to historical traditions, current developments, and issues in all contexts

    J. Reasoning to compare and contrast proposals related to contemporary social issues

X—Civic Ideals and Practices (democracy)

    A. Key ideals of democratic republican government (human dignity, liberty, justice, equality, rule of law)

    B. Sources and examples of the rights and responsibilities of citizens

    C. Multiple points of view regarding location, access, analyses, organization, and application of information on public issues

    D. Civic discussion and participation consistent with ideals of citizens in a democratic republic

    E. Citizen actions that influence public policy decisions

    F. Roles of formal and informal political actors in influencing and shaping public policy and decision making

    G. Diverse forms of public opinion on the development of public policy and decision making

   H. Effectiveness of selected public policies and citizen behaviors in realizing the stated ideals of democratic republican form of government
   I. Relationships between policy statements and action plans used to address issues of public concern through diverse strategies designed to strengthen the "common good"

FOLLOW AN INTEGRATED UNIT OF LEARNING

The Industrial Revolution serves as a model for integrated instruction in Table 3.1. Note how each core performance indicator and respective subject area contributes to the unit in this example.

DEMONSTRATE HOLISTIC INSTRUCTION

The other five performance indicators extend social studies holistically beyond core areas. They are: I—Culture and Cultural Diversity (anthropology); IV—Individual Human Development and Identity (Psychology); V—Individuals, Groups, and Institutions (sociology); VIII—Science, Technology, and Society (Social Science Education); and IX—Global Connections and Interdependence (Global Education). The performance indicators for thematic strands I, IV, V, VIII, and IX include:

   I—Culture and Cultural Diversity (anthropology)
   A. Human needs and concerns
   B. Diverse perspectives and frames of reference
   C. Contributions to the development and transmission of culture
   D. Different responses to physical and social environments and changes through shared and unique assumptions, values and beliefs
   E. Implications of cultural diversity within and across groups

Table 3.1   Sample of Integrated Unit With Core Performance Indicators

Social Studies Core Indicators	Performance Expectations	Examples
Essential Understanding or Big Idea/Topic	Specific Objective or Anticipated Outcome	Revolution/Industrial Revolution of the 1920s
II. Time, Continuity, and Change (history)	Explain, analyze, and connect patterns	Changes in U.S. businesses begun in the 1800s in attitudes and approaches toward working and living
III. People, Places, and Environments (geography)	Show physical and cultural patterns and interactions	Changes in where and how people lived, worked, invested, and spent leisure time
VI. Power, Authority, and Governance (civics/ government/ political science)	Identify role of technology that contributes to and helps resolve conflict	Changes due to Industrial Revolution, economic power, government bureaucracy, university educations, labor policies, and cultural perspectives
VII. Production, Distribution, and Consumption (economics)	Give choices related to goods and services, production, and distribution	Changes in attitudes and approaches toward capitalism, earning, investing, and spending
X. Civic Ideals and Practices (democracy)	State sources and examples of the rights and responsibilities of citizens	Changes in attitudes and approaches toward the rights of the worker

SOURCE: Adapted from National Council for the Social Studies (1994).

IV—Individual Human Development and Identity (psychology)
   A. Personal changes to social, cultural, and historical contexts
   B. Personal connections to place
   C. Personal affiliations and contributions to personal identity
   D. Physical capabilities learning, personality, and perception related to development

    E. Cultural influence on individuals' daily lives

    F. Influence of perception, dispositions, values, and beliefs on identity

    G. Examples of stereotyping, conformity, and altruism

    H. Independent and cooperative work toward goals

V—Individuals, Groups, and Institutions (sociology)

    A. Key concepts that describe the interactions of individuals and social groups

    B. Group and institutional influences on people, events, and elements of culture

    C. Forms institutions take and the interactions of people with institutions

    D. Tensions between individual and group efforts toward social conformity

    E. Tensions between belief systems and government policies and laws

    F. Roles of institutions in furthering both continuity and change

    G. Individual needs and the common good

VIII—Science, Technology, and Society (social science education)

    A. Influence of culture on scientific and technological choices and advancement

    B. People's perceptions of the social and natural world

    C. Values, beliefs, and dispositions influenced by scientific and technological knowledge

    D. Laws and policies that govern science and technological applications

    E. Reasonable and ethical solutions to problems when science and society conflict

IX—Global Connections and Interdependence (global education)

    A. Cultural elements that prompt global understanding and misunderstanding

    B. Examples of conflict, cooperation, and interdependence

    C. Effects of changing technologies

    D. Causes, consequences, and solutions to persistent, contemporary, and emerging issues

E. Relationships and tensions between national sovereignty and global interest in territory, natural resources, trade, technology, and welfare

F. Concerns, standards, issues, and conflicts related to universal human rights

G. Roles of international and multinational organizations

EXPAND THE INTEGRATED UNIT OF LEARNING

The five disciplines extend the core areas. A sample of an integrated unit using the additional performance indicators and subject areas about North American Native Americans is found in Table 3.2.

AIM FOR HIGHER-ORDER THINKING

A veteran teacher notes: *"I draw parallels between what is being discussed and the students' personal experiences. I show students that 'politics' is a part of every group to which they belong (family, choir, etc.) The fog starts to lift."*

You can make each of the social studies performance indicators come alive to enrich your instruction through higher-order thinking. Social studies teachers who design instruction conducive to higher-order thinking:

- Organize their classrooms as learning communities with student-centered seating arrangements, spacious well-equipped working centers, and flexible grouping patterns (review Chapter 1)
- Build upon national, state, and school district curricular standards and academic expectations (see Chapter 2)
- Align curriculum and instruction with authentic and alternative assessments that help the learning make sense to their students (see Chapter 4)
- Develop project-based learning and problem-solving assignments so students have a voice in the planning, choice in the investigation, and participation in the expression, reflection, and assessment (see Chapter 5)

Table 3.2   Sample of Integrated Unit With Additional Performance
                  Indicators

Social Studies Core Indicators	*Performance Expectations*	*Examples*
Essential Understanding or Big Idea/Topic	*Specific Objective or Anticipated Outcome*	*Culture/North American Native Americans*
I. Culture and Cultural Diversity (anthropology)	Describe diverse perspectives and frames of reference	Attitudes and interactions held by Native Americans and non–Native Americans throughout time
IV. Individual Human Development and Identity (psychology)	Identify personal affiliations and contributions to personal identity	Influences that Native American cultures have on individuals (both Native Americans and non–Native Americans) among and between groups
V. Individuals, Groups, and Institutions (sociology)	Analyze tensions between belief systems and government policies and laws	Impact of conflicts between various Native American belief systems and U.S. government laws
VIII. Science, Technology, and Society (social science education)	Explain people's perceptions of the social and natural world	Beliefs of Native Americans in comparison and contrast to mainstream U.S. beliefs and practices
IX. Global Connections and Interdependence (global education)	Give examples of conflict, cooperation, and interdependence	Description of the roles Native Americans' play in contemporary perceptions

SOURCE: Adapted from National Council for the Social Studies (1994).

- Include literacy that is both convergent (finding commonalities) and divergent (examining possibilities); inductive (parts to whole) and deductive (whole to parts) (see Chapter 6)
- Connect social studies themes with concepts and skills (see Chapter 7)
- Motivate ownership, encourage risk-taking, collaborate in the learning, and connect learning with living (see Chapter 9)

- Ask probing questions using Bloom's *Taxonomy of Cognitive Thinking* (1984) and Marzano and Kendall's *The New Taxonomy of Educational Objectives* (2007) (see below)

REFERENCE TWO TAXONOMIES TO WRITE OBJECTIVES

A taxonomy is an arrangement of terms that classifies concepts in a way that helps users comprehend their meaning. Traditionally, educators have referenced Bloom's Taxonomy (1984) to categorize levels of learning into three domains: cognitive (thinking), psychomotor (physical) and affective (feeling). These three domains correspond to the three common components of learning: knowledge, skills, and dispositions. During the 1980s, research on Bloom's taxonomy revealed than an updated version with emphasis on reasoning and problem-solving needed to be published. Addressing these needs is *The New Taxonomy of Educational Objectives*, authored by Marzano and Kendall in 2007. Both taxonomies provide hierarchical organizations of thinking and inquiry that equip educators to state objectives and ask questions from various levels of thought and analysis. Each taxonomy can be applied to curriculum development, instructional practices, assessment articulation, and program evalution.

FEATURE ACTIONS WITH VERBS FROM BLOOM'S TAXONOMY

Bloom's Taxonomy presents a framework that features six levels of cognitive processes: Knowledge, Comprehension, Application, Analysis, Synthesis, and Evaluation. See Table 3.3 for a description of each level and examples of verbs associated with each level.

USE THE MARZANO AND KENDALL NEW TAXONOMY

Marzano and Kendall's New Taxonomy presents a model or theory of human thought that also features six levels of processing, four cognitive levels, a meta-cognitive level, which includes setting and achieving goals, and self-system thinking, which includes motivation and attention. Table 3.4 shows the relation of Bloom's Taxonomy to the New Taxonomy.

Table 3.3   Suggested Verbs to Accompany Bloom's Taxonomy

Key verbs to guide activities and assignments or to start questions during conversations	
Evaluation: Determining the value of something	appraise, argue, assess, choose, compare, conclude, contrast, critique, debate, decide, defend, dispute, estimate, evaluate, grade, interpret, judge, justify, measure, opinionate, prioritize, prove, rank, rate, recommend, select, solve, support, validate, value, verify
Synthesis: Putting something together in a new way	arrange, change, combine, compile, compose, construct, create, derive, design, find an unusual way, forecast, formulate, generalize, generate, group, hypothesize, imagine, improve, integrate, invent, modify, organize, originate, plan, predict, pretend, produce, rearrange, reconstruct, relate, reorganize, revise, suggest, summarize, suppose, visualize, write
Analysis: Taking something apart	analyze, arrange, break down, calculate, categorize, chart, classify, compare, contrast, debate, deduct, detect, determine the factors, diagnose, diagram, differentiate, discriminate, dissect, distinguish, examine, infer, investigate, outline, relate, research, separate, show alike and different, solve, specify, subdivide, survey, test
Application: Using what you know in a new situation	act out, apply, change, collect, compute, conclude, construct, demonstrate, determine, draw, employ, exemplify, find out, give examples, illustrate, make, operate, paint, practice, predict, prepare, put in order, record, relate, report, show, solve, state a rule or principle, use
Comprehension: Understanding	change, classify, compare, convert, contrast, describe, discuss, distinguish, estimate, explain, find, generalize, give examples, give main idea, infer, interpret, paraphrase, put in order, reason, restate, retell in your own words, review, rewrite, show, summarize, trace, translate, "why"
Knowledge: Remembering	choose, count, define, describe, fill in the blank, identify, label, list, locate, match, memorize, name, outline, point out, quote, recall, recite, recognize, relate, remember, repeat, report, reproduce, select, spell, state, tell, trace, underline, "who, what, when, where"

SOURCE: Adapted from Bloom (1984).

Table 3.4   New Taxonomy, Six Levels of Processing

Six Levels of Processing	Definitions		Features	Relationship to Bloom
1. Retrieval (cognitive system)	Recognition	Recall		Knowledge
2. Comprehension (cognitive system)	Integration	Symbolism		Comprehension
3. Analysis (cognitive system)	Extension	Generation		Analysis
			A. Matching	
			B. Classifying	
			C. Analyzing errors	
			D. Generalizing	
			E. Specifying	
4. Knowledge Utilization (cognitive system)	Application	Accomplishment		Application
			A. Decision making	
			B. Problem solving	
			C. Experimenting	
			D. Investigating	
5. Meta-Cognitive System	Monitor	Control		Synthesis
			A. Specifying goals	
			B. Monitoring processes	
			C. Monitoring clarity	
			D. Monitoring accuracy	
6. Self-System Thinking	Motivation	Attention		Evaluation
			A. Examining importance	
			B. Examining efficacy	
			C. Examining response	
			D. Examining motivation	

SOURCE: Marzano and Kendall (2007).

The six levels are divided into three domains of knowledge: Information, Mental Procedures, and Psychomotor Procedures to create a two-dimension graphic organizer. Each of these domains is further divided into two categories—organizing ideas and details for Information, with processes and skills for both Mental Procedures, and Psychomotor Procedures.

From a new teacher, *"I know how much I liked social studies classes that made me think, to be able to defend my thoughts and beliefs, and to see the world differently. I want to use the same kinds of thinking skills to challenge my students."*

CAPITALIZE ON THE MULTIPLE INTELLIGENCES

You enrich your social studies instruction when you incorporate Gardner's (1983) eight multiple intelligences to examine social studies concepts, practices, and contexts. See Table 3.5 for applications to social studies. Gardner tells us that people learn and express their learning in eight different ways. Each of us has a preferred way of learning and expressing ourselves. Teachers need to be aware of their students' strengths and capitalize on them to help their students learn social studies and show optimum achievement.

Over time effective teachers include all eight of the multiple intelligences as students grow and learn from opportunities to build upon their weaker areas. As teachers design their learning experiences, they balance times when students have choice with times when students must try new avenues of learning and expression. Ultimately all students need to increase competency and confidence in learning and expressing themselves in all eight multiple intelligences.

A new teacher explains: *"One of my most successful assignments was a Metaphorical Time Line leading up to the start of World War I. The students were to create a visual metaphor to represent the events leading up to the start of World War I, with a formal essay on the back explaining all of the events. This assignment was successful because the students were able to explain the events through the visual as well as the written format. Students who are more artistic were able to dive into the project and they were then able to use that visual to help*

Table 3.5   Gardner's Multiple Intelligences Connected to Social Studies

Type of Multiple Intelligence	Examples	Social Studies Applications
Verbal linguistic/word smart: Ability to understand order, multiple meanings, and messages of words	Reading, writing, speaking, listening: Accounts, books, diaries, journals, plays, presentations, readers' theater, research, speeches, stories	Books, signs, posters, newspapers, primary and secondary source documents, reference materials
Visual spatial/picture smart: Ability to perceive the world accurately and to manipulate the nature of space	Art, charts, color, graphs, graphic organizers, illustrations, patterns, photographs, pictures, symbols, visualizing	Maps, atlases, globes, charts, graphs, graphic organizers, photographs, illustrations, art
Logical mathematical/logic smart: Ability to reason with numbers and to recognize patterns and orders	Attributes, data, logic, manipulatives, maps, measuring, money, numbers, problems, puzzles, reasoning, time, tools	Time lines of eras, centuries, lengths of time; presentations of statistics, percents, data, amounts, quantities, and totals
Bodily kinesthetic/body smart: Ability to use the body and to handle objects skillfully	Activities, body awareness, creative movement, crafts, dance, drama, experiments, field trips, investigations	Tours of museums and historical sites, industrial operations simulations, dance and creative movement
Musical rhythmic/music smart: Ability to replicate and appreciate pitch, melody, rhythm, and tone	Background music, form, instruments, moods, patterns, poetry, rhythms, songs	Of the times, about past people, and events, musical genres, instruments, voices
Interpersonal/people smart: Ability to understand people and relationships	Brainstorming, clubs, conflict resolution, consensus, cooperative learning, discussions, group work, peer editing, sharing, social awareness,	Problem identification and solving, decision making and democratic process, oral histories, service learning projects

Intrapersonal/self-smart: Ability to assess one's emotions as a means to understand and appreciate oneself, others, and society	Goal setting, choice, individual expression, individual reading, responses, reflections, self-efficacy, self-esteem, self-sufficiency	Personal connections and reflections, opinions, perspectives, and points of view autobiographies
Naturalist/nature smart: Ability to recognize and appreciate flora and fauna	Awareness of nature and natural living, balance of nature and human, community, movement, sensory experiences	Connections with outdoors, care of environment, environmental topics and issues

SOURCE: Adapted from Gardner (1983).

them write the essay. The visual metaphor served as an outline for the essay."

We also want to point out that teachers need to be aware of their own strengths and which multiple intelligences they tend to rely on and use most frequently. Teachers may be surprised to discover that they tend to teach through the same multiple intelligences, thus limiting their students' learning opportunities and choices. Armstrong (1994) suggests that each of us makes a "Multiple Intelligence Pizza." Draw a large circle and divide it into eight pieces like the slices of a pizza. Label each pizza slice as: self-smart, word smart, logic smart, people smart, music smart, body smart, picture smart, and nature smart. Describe a way you are smart that matches each pizza slice. For example, for self-smart you may know that you have a good and clear sense of yourself. Then assemble your pizza for a total view of your intelligences or strengths.

Making this pizza incorporates your own words and meanings to describe concepts you understand and value. This exercise allows you to evaluate yourself to see the whole picture of your personality and become aware of areas that you may want to fortify so that you can teach holistically to meet the needs and interests of all of your students. Your students will enjoy doing this activity too in order to become aware of their own multiple intelligences.

INCORPORATE INSTRUCTION THAT WORKS

Marzano, Pickering, and Pollock (2001) have identified nine research-based strategies that will help you maximize your social studies instruction. The nine strategies include:

1. Setting Objectives and Providing Feedback—Write your objectives to be focused and specific with clear expectations, conditions, and criterion, yet flexible to allow learners to make personal connections; feedback should be specific, positive, and helpful

2. Generating and Testing Hypotheses—Formulate hypothese to be approached inductively or deductively, be explained thoroughly, with clear conclusions

3. Providing Cues, Questions, and Advance Organizers—Use cues and questions to focus on key ideas, emphasize higher-level thinking, and allow time for students to think and respond; graphic organizers help learners manage disorganized information in their own ways

4. Summarizing and Note Taking—Summarize with learners to select information worth knowing, analyze information deeply, and be aware of the explicit context for meaning and understanding the text

5. Identifying Similarities and Differences—Reinforce with explicit modeling, guided assistance, and direct applications to graphic organizers

6. Using Nonlinguistic Representations—Select nonlinguistic representations to extend many different topics and issues, activate learners' prior knowledge and experiences, and introduce new concepts and practices that are mental, physical, and kinesthetic

7. Facilitating Cooperative Learning—Form learning groups that are small and short term; compose membership of diverse learners (Slavin, 1995), and provide clear guidelines to students

8. Designing Homework and Practice—Assign homework to increase as learners age, be completed independently from parents, have clear purposes and guidelines, and be assessed; teachers must

establish a clear homework policy for increasing student understanding and application as students master a particular skill or outcome

9. Reinforcing Effort and Providing Recognition—Reinforce effort specifically, positively, and authentically; rewards should bolster intrinsic motivation, should relate to a standard of performance, and be tangible.

These nine strategies can be used throughout your units and lesson plans in every part of your social studies curriculum and instruction. It is up to you to determine when and how you will integrate them.

An experienced teacher discusses how she uses three of these strategies on a regular basis: *"These strategies are easy to use. Students benefit immensely from knowing the objectives on which they will be tested and from the use of graphic organizers to guide their study. It gives me confidence to say that research shows these strategies, including homework, improve student achievement. The students react more willingly, too, though they still complain about homework!"*

DIFFERENTIATE INSTRUCTION

Teachers must be uniquely aware of the students in their classrooms as well as the content they are delivering (Tomlinson & McTighe, 2006). By taking time to get to know them, teachers become aware of their students' strengths, their dreams, and how to support their learning. With the diversity of learners in today's classrooms, teachers must find ways to not only identify what will be taught and assessed, but also the processes and procedures that will facilitate learning by all. It is especially important to recognize that while goals will be addressed by everyone, students may complete different tasks with different materials under different time constraints. Differential learning hinges on asking students the big essential questions that can be answered by everyone in different ways. Everyone gains not only new information but new ways of learning through individual expression of ideas and opinions (Tomlinson, 1999).

For example: You can ask students to describe the most influential person of the last 1,000 years. This individual could be famous or infamous. Your students must (1) find three facts about their selected individual and be ready to share the three facts aloud in class; (2) bring their source of information or a copy of their information; and (3) display an item or a picture of an item for which their selected individual is known. All three items must be prepared for permanent display in the classroom. Students may work independently or with others as long as each student has one individual to share.

You will have students who share information and artifacts or pictures of artifacts representative of many different countries and times because there is no right or wrong response, and you have given your students choices in how they share and display their information. We think that you will be amazed at the freedom your students will experience from this type of assignment.

Differentiated instruction includes responsive environments and flexible grouping as well as interest-based instruction, instructional strategies targeted to varied learning abilities and varied assessment. Teachers set up routines where students move in and out of learning activities in a quiet, orderly fashion, selecting materials and partners as appropriate. Self-directed learning benefits gifted and talented students, struggling readers, English learners, students with preferred learning styles, and students with disabilities. The teacher preferably determines the assessments with the students. Effective instructional strategies meet the needs of multiple groups of learners at the same time. These include graphic organizers, learning centers, and student groupings by addressing multiple intelligences, providing a variety of materials (print and digital), and giving different homework assignments.

Social studies teachers differentiate instruction by assigning different students different reading assignments to share in various ways; letting students work together on unique projects that cover more breadth and depth of the relative topics and issues (rather than all students merely repeating information shared by the teacher); generating lists of ways from which students select a method to demonstrate their learning; and so forth. The keys to differentiated learning include working collaboratively with your students to plan the learning experiences so that many different ways are available; letting students select ways that fit them best; and expressing your understanding and appreciation of the various forms of expression. It is essential that teachers who promote differentiated learning reflect sincere acceptance of the demonstrations and students.

IMPROVE STUDENT ACHIEVEMENT

Your ultimate goal is to improve student achievement across the social studies. Researchers with Educational Research Services (1999) list ten practices supported by research. We address each of these throughout our book. Table 3.6 lists these practices with examples.

Table 3.6   Ten Research-Based Practices to Improve Student Achievement

Research-Based Practice	*Classroom Examples*
1. Appropriate Classroom Environments	Emphasizing positive and caring attitudes Making available comprehendible materials
2. Jurisprudential Teaching	Teaching about fairness Teaching in ways that are fair
3. Concept Development	Coordinating learning within themes Connecting learning to living
4. Constructivist Teaching	Making the learning student centered Letting students direct and share their learning
5. Thoughtful Classrooms	Promoting higher-order thinking Featuring challenging and engaging lessons
6. Critical Thinking	Teaching how to think Teaching to ensure multiple viewpoints
7. Effective Questioning	Asking all levels of questions Guiding students in posing key questions
8. Cognitive Prejudice Reduction	Valuing different insights and expressions Seeing the world through new views
9. Computer Technology	Accessing computers to locate information Using machines to store and produce data
10. Student Participation in the Community	Introducing the world to your students Letting your students become part of the world

SOURCE: Adapted from Educational Research (1999).

Let Your Students Teach One Another . . .

The most valuable secret we can offer in planning and facilitating your instruction is to stop doing all the work and to let your students teach one another. You want to create classroom environments that are thoughtful and caring (Newmann, 1990). Adopting this approach allows your students to talk with one another using concepts and vocabulary that are their own. When they have to teach one another, they will take ownership of the learning. You might learn from them too. This is called *reciprocal teaching and learning.* One student summarizes and shares what is learned; other students ask questions and clarify the main ideas. Together students (and teacher) can then predict future events. Reciprocal teaching and learning help solidify your learning communities and make your social studies exciting. In the next chapter we present ways to develop authentic and alternative assessments that align with your curriculum and instruction.

Suggested Activities

1. Examine a unit of learning to see how you can best incorporate all the performance indicators.

2. Select a social studies topic and write a question using each of the levels of Marzano and Kendall's New Taxonomy.

3. Think of your favorite social studies unit and design one instructional strategy featuring each of the eight multiple intelligences.

4. Identify one application for each of the nine instructional strategies that work and how you will make that strategy come alive in one of your units of learning.

CHAPTER FOUR

Align Assessments With Objectives *to Strengthen Outcomes*

O ne of the most important factors of successful teaching and learning after you identify your curriculum is to align your assessments with the objectives of your instruction and outcomes. As you plan your units of learning, you will select various types of assessments to document and report your students' growth and achievement. Your assessments will give your students, their families, and you a clear sense of progress accounting for both the learning and the teaching. Assessments should be positive and productive experiences to show how well your students have learned and how effectively you have taught.

SET GOALS, OBJECTIVES, AND EXPECTATIONS

The first task in developing units and lessons is to identify goals and objectives. Goals are the long-range outcomes, big ideas, or concepts you want your students to understand, apply, and appreciate in relationship to both learning and living. Goals are often found in your state standards and district expectations. For example, the goal may be for students to comprehend the concept of "Change over time." This goal fits with almost every theme, topic, and issue within the subject areas of civics, economics, geography, and history. Goals are brought to life through unlimited kinds of learning experiences, showcasing all kinds of important social studies knowledge, skills, and dispositions. Progress toward achieving goals is checked or measured with the accumulation of many different learning experiences and assessments during a unit of learning or grading period.

> *Example of a Goal:* Students will understand the concept of change over time.

You choose how to make the goal come alive in your classroom through an instructional plan. You begin your lesson plan for the learning experience by identifying an objective or series of objectives for each goal. Objectives are short-range, narrowly defined outcomes that you can check or measure immediately. Objectives may be listed as part of the school district's scope and sequence chart or in an established course syllabus.

As you introduce individual lessons, explain to students what they are going to learn, a purpose or reason for learning (just as you do prior to reading), and how they are going to demonstrate their learning. Objectives address learning that is cognitive or about content; psychomotor or about skills; or affective or about feelings and dispositions. It is easiest to write objectives using sentences that begin with, "The student will . . ." and follow with a verb that indicates performance, such as "define," "identify," "compare," or "solve." (See Chapter 3.)

Some administrators expect you to write the objective(s) on the board. We suggest that this expectation becomes a daily routine. By posting the objective, you and the students will have a visual reference during the lesson and everyone stays focused. Continuing our earlier example, your objective might be:

> *Example of an Objective:* The student will list five common electronic devices used during the mid-twentieth century and five updated versions of the same electronic devices used during the early twenty-first century.

Your anticipated responses for the objective include: telephones/ cell phones, stereos/iPods, typewriters/word processors, ovens/ microwaves, film cameras/digital cameras. Then you decide if students will work alone, with partners, or in small groups. You also determine how students will record and report this information. These parts of your learning experience must be developmentally appropriate and match the course and classroom context.

Next, your task is to determine how you will monitor students' progress in achieving the objective(s). You have many questions to answer and communicate to your students prior to the learning experience, such as:

- What are students going to do for their assessments?
- Why have you chosen these forms of assessment?
- How will they demonstrate learning (both the process and outcomes)?
- How will learning be assessed?
- What are the assessment criteria?
- Who will assess outcomes?
- Will assessments apply to individuals or groups or both?
- How will these assessments fit into students' overall grades for the course?

Clarify why you have chosen selected forms of assessments, how they align with objective(s), and then determine an instructional plan that will enable students to be successful. Additionally, consider if you are using a balanced variety of assessments throughout the unit, semester, and year.

Example of an Assessment: *Students will work with a partner to write a magazine article on the changing role of electronic devices in daily life. The article will include two pictures, an interview with a parent/ guardian, and a time line. Students will be assessed with a rubric. Each student will receive a grade, which will be equal to a test grade.*

START WITH THE END IN MIND

When you have your assessments in mind, you will be able to select instructional strategies to ensure student success. Wiggins and McTighe (2006) promote this concept of "backward design" in planning:

1. Identify your objectives, the exact social studies knowledge, skills, and dispositions that you want your students to demonstrate at the completion of the learning experience.

2. Select how students will demonstrate their outcomes; you will have to modify expectations for various kinds of learners.

3. Decide the assessment criteria or levels of proficiency that are anticipated as satisfactory and unsatisfactory; you may have one or a set of criteria that you cluster into a rubric.

4. Organize the instruction that needs to precede the assessment.

See *Understanding by Design, Expanded, 2nd edition,* by Grant Wiggins and Jay McTighe for more on learning design.

Assessment is more than a test score to record in your grade book and send home on a report card. During a unit of learning, social studies assessments should incorporate four significant areas that include:

- Higher-order thinking
- Deep knowledge
- Substantive conversations
- Meaningful connections to the world beyond the classroom

Let's look at another example.

> *Goal: You want your students to show they know the five countries around the world with the largest populations and their economic ties to the United States.*

Working backwards, you design the teaching and learning so that students can demonstrate successful achievement. You decide to ask students what they think are the five countries and their major resources; to form investigative cooperative learning groups to look at the materials you have made available; to answer key questions about a country, its resources, and how it is linked economically to the United States; and to share reports in thirty minutes. Then you give each student a sheet of paper with a world map printed on it and a package of colored pencils. Students will outline the five countries and draw icons to represent resources that economically connect the two countries.

You also inform the students that they will be taking a written multiple-choice test on a specific upcoming date asking them to select the countries and discuss the economic links. The questions may cover all levels of knowledge as identified in Bloom's Taxonomy and Marzano and Kendall's Taxonomy. Write a sample assessment item on the board or overhead transparency so students understand the content and format of the assessment. You can show them the questions in advance if you feel it would be helpful for the students to be successful. You must decide what is developmentally appropriate for your students.

> **Objective:** *Students will identify the location of five countries with the greatest populations and describe their economic relations with the United States.*

> **Assessment:** *Brainstorm lists of countries with economic ties to the United States, brief reports on a country, creation of a products map, and a ten-question, multiple-choice test based on a map.*

This combination of assessments measures higher-order thinking, deep knowledge, substantive conversations, and meaningful connections to the world beyond the classrooms. Your assessments are organized, offer alternatives, draw content and processes from disciplines, and are elaborated through written communications. By sending work home to be shared with parents, you have reached an audience beyond the school.

FEATURE ALL THREE TYPES OF ASSESSMENT

Assessment can be divided into three categories based on when it takes place and its purpose: entry level, formative, and summative.

Entry level takes place before or at the beginning of a unit to see if students have mastered the prerequisite knowledge and skills. Checking prior learning and experiences informs you if it will be necessary to integrate any background content or skill development. It also tells you whether your students already have specific knowledge and skills that you do not have to reteach in-depth. Entry-level assessment can be written or oral or a combination of both.

> **Entry level assessment** might take place by the teacher asking students to brainstorm what they think the five largest countries by population are and what products they produce.

Formative assessment takes place during instruction and informs you of the degree to which students are progressing. Examples of formative assessment include checking for understanding by monitoring student work as it is completed in class or as homework. One way is to ask questions as you present new material or demonstrate a new skill to make sure students comprehend what you are talking about or showing. Student responses might also be in the form of showing you answers on individual whiteboards, writing a summary at the end of a lesson for you to read, completing a graphic organizer to submit for your review, or taking a quiz.

> **Formative assessment** takes place as the teacher monitors the progress of the research on the countries and the presentations. In addition, the teacher checks the product maps the students are creating.

Summative assessment takes place at the end of a unit. Examples of summative assessment include a unit test or an alternative assessment, such as a poster, report, or performance. You will not be able to use all the various types of assessments for any given unit, but over the course of a semester or year, you can offer students a variety of assessment experiences. Remember, the more types you employ, the greater the variety of opportunities you give the students to demonstrate their achievements.

> **Summative assessment** takes place as the teacher evaluates the maps and the multiple-choice test.

On a given day, you may use one, two, or all three types of assessment (entry-level, formative or progress-monitoring, and summative). During a unit of instruction, you will use all three. While there may be assessments based on group or whole class responses, ultimately there should be some individual summative assessment (Bol & Strange, 1996).

DETERMINE THE FUNCTIONS AND PURPOSES

Assessment is the process by which students demonstrate five functions of and purposes for learning (Stiggins, 2005):

1. Knowledge and understanding: Answers the questions of who, what, and where.

2. Logic and reasoning: Answers the questions of why, why not, and how do you know.

3. Skills and demonstration: Answers the questions of how and can you show me.

4. Productivity and creativity: Answers the questions of what else and how might you do this or do this differently

5. Outlooks and dispositions: Answers the questions of what you think is important, how you feel, and how someone else might think or feel.

You want to include assessments that provide feedback on all five functions either independently of one another or in combination with other functions. For example, you may want your students to demonstrate knowledge only. Or you may want your students to demonstrate a combination of knowledge and skill. It is essential that you are clear about your expectations before you determine what you want your students to demonstrate. Then select the structure or format as described in the next section.

VARY THE STRUCTURES AND FORMATS

Assessment is not as overwhelming as many teachers might believe. Let's look at four general structures and formats that you want to incorporate into your assignments and feedback (Stiggins, 2005): *selected responses, constructed essays, demonstrated performances,* and *personal communications.* Again, you will want to create outcomes that utilize all four types of structures either independently or in combination with the other structures. For example, you can develop an assessment with only selected responses, such as multiple-choice, or you can create an assessment with both selected responses, such as true/false; and constructed essays, such as short answers.

The more important aspects of designing assessments are (1) to align the assessment with the curriculum and instruction so the objective matches the assessment, and (2) to be sure the assessment measures what you want to measure, such as if you want to know if your students can produce a reasoned argument, then ask your students to write a constructed essay to a question they can prepare for and answer intelligently. And (3) you want your assessment to be developmentally appropriate. Your assessments will be an opportunity for your students to showcase their learning. The assessments allow them chances to do well and for students to feel good about their accomplishments. Assessments are not a time to surprise students or to make them feel inadequate.

USE SELECTED RESPONSES

Selected responses sounds just like the name; students pick the answer from a prepared written group (usually a list) of items. Selected responses include multiple-choice, matching, true/false, fill-in-the-blank, or checklists. Selected responses are the most-liked assessment by most students because the answers are given to them. Students simply have to pick one of the responses; they do not have to think or remember or analyze or connect. Through the process of elimination, students can narrow their choices to a few items and make their best guess. There is no reason for a student to not complete this form of assessment because the student can always take a chance on getting the right answer.

Selected responses also are the most liked by most teachers because they are quick and easy to grade. You can make an answer key or template; often times you use a Scantron machine to do the checking. You can give a selected response exam one day and return it the next day, even when you assess five or six sections of the same course in one day. Plus, you can mix up the order of questions quite easily to create five or six different versions of the same test, giving a different version of the same exam to each section of the same course. This prevents students from memorizing the order of answers by their initials and sharing the answers with friends throughout the day.

However, writing a selected response assessment is not as easy as it might appear. Craft the wording of the statements carefully to avoid ambiguity and confusion. You may find yourself writing selected response statements identical to phrases you have spoken in class, written on overheads, and/or distributed in notes and assignments. You want to consider if your selected response assessment is just asking for recognition of vocabulary and concepts or do students have to think about application.

Many of the assessments that accompany your textbooks rely primarily on various forms of selected responses. The questions usually contain the same vocabulary as presented in the textbook and frequently in much the same way. However, make sure the language of the test bank is the same as the language of the text, as sometimes they are written by different authors.

INCLUDE CONSTRUCTED ESSAYS

Constructed essays include written words, sentences, and paragraphs originating from the student's memory. They can vary in format from a traditional essay to a creative exercise, such as a newspaper article, editorial, or letter. They are probably the least-liked form of assessment by most students and most teachers. These assessments take time to write, time to complete, and time to check.

Not only must you prepare your students thoroughly to know the main ideas and supportive examples, but your students must also be able to connect the main ideas and communicate their thoughts coherently.

Students will want to know exactly how they are going to be graded; therefore, detailed rubrics accounting for inclusion of information and presentation of ideas need to be developed in advance. Rubrics also enable you to give your students credit if your students' answers are not complete. You also must be prepared to give a student credit if the answer is different from the usual or anticipated response. Finally, you need to decide if you will assess the English language development as well as the social studies development.

From a veteran teacher: *"I used multiple-choice all the time when I started teaching. Now I know how to balance my assessments and let the students make more choices that fit their needs and interests."*

HIGHLIGHT DEMONSTRATED PERFORMANCES

Demonstrated performances include actions and presentations shown to an individual or to a group (either spontaneously or prepared), frequently integrating constructed essays and personal communications. They can be quick and easy or much longer and more involved. For example, asking a student to point to a location on a map, salute the flag during the Pledge of Allegiance, or give a speech are all demonstrated performances. They also include much more involved presentations, such as sharing data on a chart or graph. Other examples are singing, dancing, and acting. Art forms can be integrated into social studies easily.

> *One of the presentations I gave was on John Quincy Adams who was the second president. In the presentation I had to give full detail on his background and some of the things he achieved while in office.*

> Trevor, age 15, Grade 10

Teachers and students will likely enjoy learning how to shake hands and make introductions. The same feelings might occur when role playing or participating in a skit. However, when required to recite portions of the Preamble of the Constitution or give an oral report, students may become much more nervous and uncomfortable. Teachers can provide students with plenty of direction and support so they will understand and be able to achieve the assessment successfully. Again, teachers must prepare their students with the content and processes related to social studies with a detailed rubric of expectations. Showing a sample videotape or modeling your expectation will help guide students. Try to take time to guide your students with intellectual and emotional reassurance. Students will need time to practice. Your encouragement is vital.

From a teacher: *"One of the most successful classroom experiences is to have students select a historical figure to study and then participate in a panel discussion as though they are the figure. Students research biographies and autobiographies and then select what they feel are the salient positions in their figures' lives."*

There are many interactive forms of demonstrated performance. Mock trials, skits, legislative hearings, debates, panel discussions, and newscasts also fall in this category.

From another teacher: *"My students love to act in front of a camera. Students take turns videoing performances, and then we play them back and critique them. They also like to have their best examples shown to other classes so their friends can see their work!"*

Demonstrated performances allow students to showcase their knowledge, understanding, logic, reasoning, productivity, and creativity with skills that may be new to the teacher and other students. You may be surprised to discover the public speaking and intellectual demonstration talents of some of your quieter students. These are important skills to promote as many students will need them when attending universities and during their careers.

> *Oral presentations are a good way to show a teacher what you've learned. Sometimes I don't like this because I get nervous. This isn't a good thing when the presentation is worth a lot of points.*

> Maya, age 13, Grade 8

Teachers frequently ask their students to assess other students during demonstrated performances. This approach to assessment expands the audience and helps students to direct their products toward their peers. Guide students to measure peers against realistic expectations while providing positive and constructive feedback. Talk with your colleagues to determine which assignments would be appropriate for peer feedback.

REMEMBER PERSONAL COMMUNICATIONS

Personal communications are overlooked as a viable form of assessment, yet they are the most frequently used types of assessments. Personal communications include short oral answers or responses to questions or lengthier verbal explanations conducted through both formal and informal conversations. When you ask a student any kind of question and expect a verbal response, it becomes a personal communication. Your question may be related to your lesson or your question may be related to the student. Conversations may be highly structured and organized, in a panel discussion format, or a prepared list of questions related to the textbook, or your conversations may be more spontaneous as when you use the Socratic Method.

You probably are not formally grading your students during personal communications; however, you are assessing their responses in the moment to confirm understanding. You decide if a student or a group of students, perhaps the entire class, comprehends an idea allowing you to move to the next idea or if you need to revisit and reteach the idea. Every teacher does this every day. This is a form of progress monitoring or formative assessment mentioned above.

From a fifth-year teacher: *"I rely heavily upon personal communications conducted in class. I ask all kinds of questions and listen carefully to the students' responses. This way I know if most of the students understand the lesson and are ready to move on."*

OFFER AUTHENTIC AND ALTERNATIVE ASSESSMENTS

Although tests test your knowledge, some people aren't very good at taking tests. The best way would probably be a project—something big, when you have to spend a lot of time on it. This requires you to actually learn something.

Kim, age 15, Grade 10

Many teachers tend to use the same types of assessments over and over. Like teaching methods, however, assessment techniques are unlimited. The secret to success is to select a variety of alternative assessments that fits assignments authentically and helps connect the learning to the real world. For example, to learn the spelling words, your students can spell the words aloud to a partner; they can write the words on paper, or with markers on the board or on an overhead transparency; you can organize a spelling bee; the students can write the words on the computer and use spell-check for feedback; they could teach another student how to spell and use the new words; or they could select which word is spelled either correctly or incorrectly in a sentence or story. Ultimately, the students could write the sentence or story themselves and exchange papers with one another. Be thoughtful and creative. Another authentic assessment would be for students to write articles for a student magazine or newspaper.

Authentic assessments are based on work that is produced for a real audience or is carried out in a real-world context. Tomlinson and McTighe (2006) suggest several examples appropriate for social studies. They include, conducting research using primary sources, debating a controversial issue, solving "real-world" problems, and writing purposefully for an audience. Plan for your students to do documentary-type activities that involve writing, photography, audio taping, and videotaping, along with interviewing. Other examples of authentic work and authentic assessment include service learning projects and active citizenship projects. (See Chapter 11.)

INCORPORATE PORTFOLIOS

Portfolio assessments have students demonstrate what they have learned. With portfolios, students select the best examples of their work—an assortment of documents relating to a particular social studies theme (Council of Chief State School Officers, 2001). They can also be asked to evaluate their selections and write a brief reflection on the significance of each piece that is included. Here are some examples of themes in the different subject areas:

- Civics—citizenship, governments, governance, international relationships
- Economics—choice, interdependence, markets, resources, systems

- Geography—cultures, environment, physical systems, places, regions
- History—changes, continuity, developments, interactions, technology

Portfolio documents should represent a variety of the following: thorough description, valid interpretation, balanced research, rigorous investigation, structured analysis, productive problem solving, reasoned persuasion, and critical implications. Portfolio rubrics address:

1. Content evidence, description, and support

2. Skills and processes relevant to the content

3. Conceptual understanding connecting content and processes to life

4. Articulation, communication, and presentation of portfolio

Portfolio assessment allows you to delve into your students' thinking, understanding, logic, reasoning, plus outlooks and dispositions extremely well. When you ask for strongly developed constructed essays, you can assess your students' abilities to give a clear and succinct explanation, contextualization, or connection that reflects your best teaching.

PREPARE A SCORING PLAN

With selected responses, the scoring is straightforward. Answers are correct or incorrect. With constructed essays, demonstrated performances, and personal communications, you will find that checklists, rating scales, or rubrics facilitate the assessment process.

Rubrics or scoring guides identify the criteria for the characteristics of the product or skills that will be evaluated and how the grade will be determined. Rubrics include knowledge and skills; degree of proficiency or whether a behavior is observed or not; use of required procedures; demonstrations of dispositions; and exhibitions of social skills (Borich & Tombari, 2003). Scoring can be holistic and give an overall evaluation of student work or it can be analytically based on specific identified behaviors and traits of students' knowledge, skills, and dispositions. Both students and parents appreciate such detailed information. The mystery is taken out of grading as it becomes more objective. Students can be involved in creating the rubrics and can self-evaluate their work based on what has been developed. You will also find that rubrics enable you to grade student work more quickly and return it in a timely way.

UNDERSTAND THE RESULTS OF STANDARDIZED TESTING

Standardized testing, a form of summative assessment, is the focus of many discussions both in schools and throughout society. You may have mixed feelings about standardized testing. We all need to know that what is being taught is indeed being learned. We all need to know that the majority of students have achieved the goals of a particular grade level and/or subject area and are ready for the next level. As teachers, we want to know if our methods of teaching are effective and help our students to succeed. As the data from standardized testing become available, the results will be given to you to make improvements in your teaching and your students' learning.

Criterion-referenced tests are designed to measure what students have learned against a set of standards (criteria), such as the district objectives. They are locally developed. The tests you give at the end of a semester, for example, will likely be criterion-referenced tests. Your district may have quarterly exams. This type of test tells you whether or not your students have mastered identified objectives. You receive specific feedback from this kind of evaluation. You will see how well your students did and whether any gaps exist that you will need to address. This information will enable you to identify areas for reteaching.

Norm-referenced tests measure students against like students, usually across the nation. For example, the achievement of a second-semester, "Grade X" student in your school is compared to all second-semester, "Grade X" students who took the test. These are the tests that are being used as the basis for school accountability today.

You will receive information on how students did on various tasks included in the test; however, information from the task analysis tends to be general rather than specific. Also, these tests are highly dependent on reading ability, which can be a problem for many students. Unfortunately, there is often a lag time of weeks or months between the date the test is submitted for scoring and the date the received results are shared with teachers.

Check your district and school calendars for dates of mandated standardized testing. You may also do pre- and post-testing of grade level skills at the beginning and end of each year along with regular benchmark progress monitoring along the way. Some assessments are given to the entire class at one time; others are given individually.

DEVELOP AN ASSESSMENT BLUEPRINT

As you developed a year-long plan to cover your standards as suggested in Chapter 2, you can record an assessment plan. Plot your summative assessments over the course of the year so that students have the opportunity to experience many different kinds of assessments, including tests, projects, and performances. Incorporate your students' learning styles and multiple intelligences. Explore with students which types of assessments they think are the most fun and engaging. A list of additional alternative and authentic assessments is found in Box 4.1.

Then, within each unit, identify what type of entry-level assessment you will use to find out what content and skills the students already possess. Throughout the unit, plan formative assessment activities and conclude with summative activities that address your objectives.

Make Sure the Process Makes Sense for Everyone . . .

Align your curriculum and assessments so they make sense to you and your students. We recommend that you approach your planning holistically so these components are well developed long in advance

Box 4.1 A to Z of Authentic and Alternative Assessments

Advertisement, artifact replicas, animated stories

Blog, brochure, bulletin board

Collage, children's and young people's books, constitution

Dance, database, debate, demonstration, diorama, drawings

Editorial

Fashion show, fishbowl discussion

Games, graphic organizers

Historical portrayal of person or event

Illustrated time line, interview

Journal entry

K-W-L chart

Legislative hearing, letter, learning log

Maps, mobiles, mock trial, model, museum

Newscast

Obituary, oral history

Photographic essay, play, podcast, poem, political cartoon, poster

Questionnaire and results analysis, quilt

Role play

Simulation, slide show, song, speech, storyboard

Television program, think-aloud, tiered time line, treaty

Unit summary with illustrations

Video documentary, virtual field trip

Web site, wikis, word wall

Xylograph (wood engraving) or other artistic rendering

Yearbook or similar type documentary

Z to A or A to Z alphabet-type presentation

SOURCE: Adapted from Kottler, Kottler, & Kottler (2004).

of your actual teaching. Be sure that you have included all structures of assessment to accomplish all the functions. With the assessments in mind, you'll be ready to take on the role of instructional leader.

Here's an important secret. As you begin teaching, remember how you felt as a student. You wanted to know how you were doing in class and the grade you were earning. You liked feedback and to be updated with each assignment. Today's students and their parents feel the same way. Announce assessments in advance and provide feedback, oral and written, to students as quickly as possible.

In the next chapter we look at how to connect the learning to reach your students' lives through exciting projects conducted in and outside the classroom. Your students will be engaged in meaningful skills they will use throughout their lives.

Suggested Activities

1. Reflect on your own social studies classes. Identify the type of assessment that was used most often, and the type of assessment that you preferred.

2. Think of one social studies objective and describe how you would assess mastery learning of that objective through selected responses, constructed essays, demonstrated performances, and personal communications.

3. From your curriculum, select one topic and make a connection between the topic and the five functions of assessment.

4. Make a list of ways you can prepare your students for standardized testing that are natural and supportive.

C H A P T E R   F I V E

Connect the Learning *to Reach Students' Lives*

We suggest that you concentrate on social studies skills or the things that students need to know how to *do* to connect the learning quickly and easily to your students' lives. This is a two-part secret. First, the more you can engage your students in actively participating in their learning, the more they will learn and the more they will enjoy the learning. Second, as you advance their learning and your students become more motivated, they will make more connections, personalize the learning, and take ownership in the outcomes.

INTEGRATE THE SIX MAJOR SOCIAL STUDIES SKILLS

In previous chapters, we examined the social studies content and instructional performance indicators related to each of the NCSS thematic strands, documenting social studies content or what students should *know*. Now let's outline social studies skills or what students should *do* as you organize all of your units and lessons.

Most social studies skills apply to all of the content areas. Skills definitely should not be fragmented or taught in isolation; they reach across the curriculum offering interconnected proficiencies for students to apply throughout the learning process. Social studies skills can be grouped into six major areas that include:

1. *Making inquiries and conducting investigations*—Promotes asking questions of interest and importance to the learner to local situations, of society, and of humanity; organizing studies to pursue inquiries to inform the learner, to provide insights on topics and issues, to clarify ideals, to expose ramifications, and to strengthen connections between the learner and the social studies concepts and processes (Levstik & Barton, 1997)

2. *Acquiring information and manipulating data*—Features observing and reading a variety of sources, talking with people, and visiting places to help make sense of the world and inform actions; social studies incorporates vocabulary, concepts, and contexts for readers to experience and comprehend all social studies literacies

3. *Developing and presenting position statements, arguments, policies, and stories*—Incorporates the writing process to practice classifying, interpreting, analyzing, summarizing, evaluating, and presenting information in well-reasoned ways that inform and support wise decision making for individuals, groups, and society (Engle & Ochoa, 1988)

4. *Constructing new knowledge, skills, dispositions, and comprehension*—Conceptualizes unfamiliar categories of information, establishing cause and effect relationships, determining the validity of information and arguments, and developing a new story, model, narrative, picture, or chart that enhances one's understanding, application, and appreciation of an event, idea, or persons

5. *Participating in groups and individually*—Includes expressing and advocating reasoned personal convictions within groups, recognizing mutual ethical responsibility in groups, participating in negotiating conflicts and differences or maintaining an individual position because of its ethical basis, working individually and in groups, and accepting and fulfilling responsibilities associated with citizenship in a democratic republic; articulating one's thoughts and beliefs (Kohn, 1997)

6. *Taking action and making a difference*—Requires committing resources and energies to selected interests and endeavors locally or globally in ways that are comfortable and constructive; strengthening connections between learning and living to improve the quality of life near and far for oneself and for others

The major skills provide an overarching framework for teaching and learning, so your next task is to identify the specific skills for your course, whether you are teaching civics and government, economics, geography, history, or social studies in general. Most states have identified specific skills as part of their state social studies standards and/or curriculum framework as well as the content goals and objectives.

According to the California International Studies Project (CISP), an easy way to group the specific skills is by organizing them into three different categories:

- Chronological and spatial thinking—Skills relating to time and space or questions of when and where
- Historical interpretation—Skills relating to issues and events or questions of what and why
- Research, evidence, point of view—Skills relating to mission and agenda or questions of who and how

As you will see in the next sections, these three categories encompass skills in geography, economics, and civics, as well as history involving researching many points of view.

NAVIGATE CHRONOLOGICAL AND SPATIAL THINKING

Start by establishing a clear understanding of time and space related with your curriculum content. These are the two skills that are most concrete and that students can grasp most easily. However, your students bring limited connections with events from long ago and far away. Keep in mind that they were born within the last ten to eighteen years and most of them probably have not traveled very far. Your students who have traveled either emigrated from another country or visited places as tourists. They may or may not have much information or understanding about their travels. You will have to inquire into your students' prior knowledge and experiences with time and space carefully.

To develop chronological and spatial thinking, give students opportunities to:

- Make and interpret time lines by placing key events and people of the historical era they are studying both in a chronological sequence and within a spatial context
- Apply terms related to time correctly, including vocabulary such as *past, present, future, decade, century, era,* and *generation*
- Explain how the present is connected to the past, identifying both similarities and differences between the two, and how some things change over time and some things stay the same (e.g., relate current events)
- Use map and globe skills to determine the absolute locations of places and interpret information available through the map's legend, scale, and symbolic representations
- Judge the significance of the relative location of a place (e.g., close to a harbor, trade routes) and analyze how those relative advantages or disadvantages can change over time
- Use a variety of maps and documents to identify physical and cultural features of neighborhoods, cities, states, and countries (e.g., to explain the historical migration of people, expansion and disintegration of empires, and the growth of economic systems)
- Explain how major events are related to one another in time
- Construct various time lines of key events, people, and periods of the historical era they are studying
- Compare and contrast the present with the past, evaluating the consequences of past events and decisions and determining the lessons that were learned
- Analyze how change happens at different rates at different times; understand that some aspects can change while others remain the same; and understand that change is complicated and affects not only technology and politics but also values and beliefs
- Use a variety of maps and other documents to interpret human movement, including major patterns of domestic and international migration, changing environmental

preferences and settlement patterns, the frictions that develop between population groups, and the diffusion of ideas, technological innovations, and goods

> **Example of Chronological and Spatial Thinking:** *Find and/or draw maps of your town or city to show growth changes in commercial, residential, and recreational properties. Indicate the economic changes shown by modifications in transportation, imports, exports, and trade over time.*

EXPLORE HISTORICAL INTERPRETATION

Time involves history and the most challenging skills are those addressing historical interpretation. Students need to develop skills for giving reasons accounting for events and outcomes. These skills are much more complex and complicated to unravel and understand. Some historical interpretations may contradict prior learning either from school, from home, or over time. Students must stay open minded and be mindful of the many different causes and effects associated with events over time.

To develop historical interpretation skills, students need opportunities to:

- Summarize the key events of the era they are studying and explain their historical contexts
- Identify the human and physical characteristics of the places they are studying and explain how these features form the unique character of these places
- Identify and interpret the multiple causes and effects of historical events
- Explain the central issues and problems from the past, placing people and events in a matrix of time and place
- Understand and distinguish cause, effect, sequence, and correlation in historical events, including the long- and short-term causal relations
- Recognize the roles of chance, oversight, and error in history
- Realize that interpretations of history are subject to change as new information is uncovered

- Interpret basic indicators of economic performance and conduct cost-benefit analyses of economic and political issues
- Show the connections, causal and otherwise, between particular historical events and larger social, economic, and political trends and developments
- Notice the complexity of historical causes and effects, including the limitations on determining cause and effect
- Interpret past events and issues within the context in which an event unfolded rather than solely in terms of present-day norms and values
- Understand the meaning, implication, and impact of historical events and recognize that events could have taken other directions

---

Example of Historical Interpretation: *Look at the contributions of the Renaissance in relationship to towns, work, education, the arts, and so forth. Divide your class into cooperative learning groups to research and share the contributions with the rest of the class.*

CONSIDER CIVIC/CITIZENSHIP ACTIVITIES

Civics or citizenship focuses on one's national identity, constitutional heritage, individual and group rights and responsibilities, global interactions and multicultural interactions, and pluralistic values. The concepts and practices encompass democratic principles, social justice, issues of equity and freedom, and so forth.

To understand civic activities, students grow from opportunities to:

- Recognize that the United States is a country of Native Americans and immigrants from around the world
- Acknowledge that the U.S. population is comprised of people from many different heritages, races, ethnicities, nationalities, and belief systems
- Realize that the U.S. population continues to change due to many different factors
- Understand that the United States is founded on rights and responsibilities of freedom, equality, tolerance, and acceptance, democracy, and patriotism

- Develop qualities of a democratic society and a participatory democracy
- Compare and contrast the structures and functions of the U.S. with other countries and changes within the U.S. over time

---

Example of Civic/Citizenship Activities: During the next state or national election, bring in copies of newspapers and news magazine articles for your students to monitor and assess the changes in public opinion related to various key issues. Ask your students to predict the winners of several elections and to substantiate their predictions with information they have gleaned from various sources. Then check the predictions.

EXAMINE ECONOMIC TRENDS

Most students and teachers seem to fear the study of economics, yet both groups greatly enjoy the practices of economics, especially when it comes to spending. Economics describes needs and wants, goods and services, trades and exchanges, sales and savings, assets and liabilities, production and consumption, manufacturing and distributing, inflation and depression, scarcity and abundance. The concepts of economics apply to items of monetary value as well as social and emotional value. If only a few samples of an item are available, the item becomes more desired and valuable. Wanting the item may be real, perceived, or conceived by marketing. As consumers, we are easily swayed by advertising and publicity in how we spend our time, money, and energy.

To understand economic trends, students benefit from opportunities to:

- Learn about various market systems including the laws regulating them
- Connect market systems with political and social systems
- Reveal shared and unique market goals, performance, and problems
- Understand the basic economic challenges facing all individuals and societies—locally and globally
- Examine the global marketplace

- Recognize the influence of the international economic system on underdeveloped, developing, and developed countries
- Participate in the market in various capacities

Example of Economic Trends: Give each of your students a sample product that is commonly found in most homes. Instruct your students to research the product's origins on the Internet so they can report where the product is grown, how much the product contributes to the welfare of the country, where the product is manufactured and the various other goods, if any, the product is used to make, how the product is transported to the U.S., the price in the U.S., the amount of consumption, and the welfare it generates in the U.S.

INVESTIGATE RESEARCH, EVIDENCE, AND POINT OF VIEW

For every social studies topic and issue, you want your students to know how to ask important questions, how to conduct reasonable investigations, where to find the most informative resources, how to weigh various conditions, how to see situations from various perspectives, and how to make wise decisions. These skills will captivate your students as they begin to realize that the social studies offers stories full of paradox, mystique, irony, and uncertainty. Through research they will discover that there may be no one right answer.

To develop research, evidence, and point of view skills, students need time to:

- Differentiate between primary and secondary sources
- Pose relevant questions about events encountered in historical documents, eyewitness accounts, oral histories, letters, diaries, artifacts, photos, maps, art, and architecture
- Distinguish fact from fiction by comparing documentary sources on historical figures and events with fictionalized characters and events
- Frame questions that can be answered by historical study and research

- Discern fact from opinion in historical narratives and stories
- Divide relevant from irrelevant information, essential from incidental information, and verifiable from unverifiable information in historical narratives and stories
- Assess the credibility of primary and secondary sources and draw sound conclusions from them
- Detect the different historical points of view on historical events and determine the context in which the historical statements were made (the questions asked, sources used, authors' perspectives)
- Separate valid arguments from fallacious arguments in historical interpretations
- Identify bias and prejudice in historical interpretations
- Construct and test hypotheses; collect, evaluate, and employ information from multiple primary and secondary sources; and apply it in oral and written presentations

> **Example of Research, Evidence, and Point of View:** *Tell your students you are inviting a guest speaker to visit your class to discuss a topic or issue related to your curriculum. You could invite someone who had been imprisoned during the Holocaust, the Japanese-American Internment, the Vietnam conflict, and so forth. Ask your students to work in cooperative learning groups to craft a list of questions and be prepared to defend their selections. Then bring the groups together to consolidate and prioritize the lists into one list of the ten most important questions.*

From a veteran teacher: *"I find lesson planning to be the most stimulating and creative aspect of teaching. I love deciding which instructional strategies and materials to use with my students. Each year I do something a little different based on last year's experiences and new ideas I've gained from talking to other teachers."*

Planning and preparation are vital to successful teaching. You have thought about arranging your classroom, and you are grounded in aligning your curriculum, objectives, and assessment. Now you are ready to consider how you will plan your instruction.

CREATE CONSTRUCTIVIST CLASSROOMS

The ideal way to engage your students in social studies skills is to create a constructivist classroom (Brooks & Brooks, 1999; Sunal & Haas, 2002). Constructivism blends two seemingly opposing approaches to education that you want to incorporate into your social studies classrooms. You need to arm your students with information and access to all kinds of facts, figures, and philosophies related to time, places, people, events, systems, and so forth. You also want to equip your students with the application and appreciation for facts, figures, and philosophies through personal connections, from multiple perspectives, and in various contexts. Furthermore, you want to enable students to analyze and evaluate information to form their own conclusions and even contribute to the field. You can achieve these goals by creating constructivist classrooms.

Constructivist teachers:

- Present curriculum whole to part with an emphasis on big ideas
- Develop curriculum around themes and issues significant to humans
- Pursue student-generated questions
- Use authentic manipulatives and reference primary sources
- Organize activities and projects as group work with diverse group members
- View students as critical thinkers with insights built on prior knowledge and experiences
- Interact with students, modeling the learning process collaboratively
- Explore students' point of view and preferred methods of expression
- Assess through observation, conversation, and demonstration

Following constructivism, teachers and students are continuously checking and revising their thoughts, words, actions, and interactions as they compare and contrast the known with the unknown in the processes of acquiring new knowledge, skills, and dispositions. Teachers help students negotiate dissonance and conflict, an aspect of essential development to support middle level, middle school, and high school students.

Example of a Constructivist Classroom: You are planning to teach a unit comparing and contrasting the current events in Iraq with the U.S. involvement in Vietnam during the 1950s, 60s, and 70s. Rather than assigning a section of the textbook to read and discuss, you could begin the unit by asking your students not only what they know about each event, but inviting them to identify what they want to know and why they want to know these particular pieces of information.

Then you could ask your students to talk with their parents, grandparents, aunts, uncles, and anyone else who might have been involved in the Vietnam events or have some information or opinions. You could show a documentary or play some of the music from that era, and invite a veteran to speak with your class.

You could continue by having students ask family and friends about the current events in Iraq and provide newspapers and news magazines for students to read to become more informed from a multitude of perspectives. Now, you could invite a current service member to speak to the class.

Finally you could discuss with students how they want to measure their learning by designing a rubric collaboratively. The rubric will determine how the students can or will express and share their learning. Many students want to be given choices that showcase their preferred learning styles. Together you and your students can also decide how to assess the learning, i.e., self-assessments, peer assessments, and/or teacher assessments, and then how to evaluate the assessments for an overall grade.

Your role becomes one of facilitating resources the students will need to answer their questions, arranging and monitoring groups, and making a time line of activities. Again, this opens the door for differentiated learning.

You will need to discuss with students how they want to measure their learning and what the assessments will look like. You will also facilitate acquiring the resources you will need to answer their questions and making a time line of activities. These approaches open the door for differentiated learning.

When you focus the learning on what your students know, what they want to learn, and their reasons for learning, you have transformed your class into one that is constructivist in nature. You let go of preconceived outcomes and focus on authentic learning that is fueled by genuine intrigue. We think that the more often you can incorporate constructivist approaches into your classes, the more your students will learn and enjoy social studies.

SELECT QUESTIONS EFFECTIVELY

Select and use questions effectively during teacher talk to stimulate student responses. There are eight main types of questions (Callahan, Clark, & Kellough, 1998). Each has a different purpose. Box 5.1 shows the eight types of questions with examples. Be deliberate in phrasing your questions to achieve your goals.

CONSIDER VARIOUS APPROACHES TO ASK QUESTIONS

There are several approaches to keep in mind when asking questions in your classroom. You can certainly write down some questions in advance of the discussion by following Marzano and Kendall's New Taxonomy as shown in Chapter 3. Or you also can look in the teacher's manual for key questions that the textbook authors may have already written for you.

When you construct your own questions, be sure that you make them easy to understand. Certainly you want to avoid confusing or overwhelming your students with the question when you are trying to get them to think and respond about the information necessary to answer the question. Too many teachers err on the side of "trying to trick" their students with double negatives or questions that either have no answers or simply can't be answered. Using these types of techniques will guarantee your students' dislike of social studies and their distrust of you.

As you ask your own questions, be open to the various directions the discussions may go. You want to be ready with additional questions to both probe deeper into a particular topic or issue, and

Box 5.1   Eight Types of Questions With Examples

Focusing—Directing attention and energy: "Who needs a copy of the map?"

Convergent Thinking—Narrowing the choices and searching for a single answer: "What would you say was the cause?"

Evaluating—Making a judgment or placing a value: "Who thinks we should change this rule and why do you think that way?"

Clarifying—Delving into associated thought processes: "Would you describe an appropriate symbol?"

Probing—Asking for additional information and examples: "How many of you recycle trash regularly?"

Cuing—Providing clues to connect with a bigger idea or concept: "What would this piece of evidence lead you to believe?"

Divergent Thinking—Broadening the choices and encouraging possibilities promoted by higher-order thinking responses: "If you could do that differently, what would you do?"

Socratic Thinking—Conducting a dialogue where students must think critically about the problem, reflecting mindfully on their individual beliefs, and applying contextually their insights igniting student interest and energies (Brogan & Brogan, 1995)

SOURCE: Adapted from Callahan, Clark, & Kellough (1998).

to expand the conversation to reflect your students' growing interests. This means you need to have extra questions prepared prior to the discussion.

Here's a suggestion: Avoid trying to "wing it," especially when you are inexperienced; and, particularly, if there is any chance at all that an administrator, department chair, colleague, or parent will be observing you. (In other words . . . every day there is a chance that this day will be one of those days.) Many of you will be teaching students who will be able to detect if you know your material and are prepared for class. You want your students to learn along with you, so have a variety of questions ready at all times as you monitor discussions so that all students have an opportunity to answer.

Another approach is to divide your students into small groups of two or more and ask them to write a few questions on different sections of the assigned reading. Give each group clear instructions as to who is leading the group, who is recording the questions, and so forth. Do not presume that your students will jump right into this type of group work and everyone will contribute. You want to monitor group progress closely.

After a specified amount of time, collect the questions, review them quickly to make sure they are appropriate, and then redistribute the questions using one of several different techniques. You can select individuals or groups, or you can allow individuals or groups to select their questions. Then you will have to decide if students have time to seek the answers, write a response, discuss their questions, or simply respond from memory. You can modify these approaches easily depending on the text and your students.

If you are teaching more than one section of the same course, you can ask the students in each section of the course to write questions to use with another section of the course. This technique will fascinate your students as they will not be in the same room with the students who wrote the questions. Now your students can analyze the questions more openly and honestly. You will experience a different kind of conversation.

There are many ways to use questioning effectively with your students. It is essential that you are ready and that you vary your approaches so your students feel comfortable and yet challenged. Keep a record of what works for you, your students, and for various social studies topics and issues. This is one area where you definitely want to succeed and where you will improve with time, practice, and experience.

From a veteran teacher: *"It's important to decide on the order and level of open-ended questions and give students plenty of time to answer them. I like to have students share answers with a partner and then ask, 'Who heard a good response?' As students hear their answers repeated, they receive peer recognition for their participation."*

ADVANCE YOUR CLASSROOM DISCUSSIONS

Most likely you will encourage your students to participate in classroom discussions every day. You want to hear what they are thinking about the reading, previous classroom discussions, and connections to various activities in your class, in other classes, and in their lives outside of class. The secret to success in your classroom discussions depends on your ability to facilitate or lead the discussions, to motivate students to participate through speaking and listening (incorporating both cognitive and emotional responses), and to link the discussions with your purposes for learning.

You can think of discussions as part of both the content and the process. That means, you can teach using discussions to explore a subject, and you can teach about having discussions as a way to articulate and exchange ideas. Each of these approaches is extremely important in the social studies. After all, social studies is the study of groups and the expression of many different ideas and beliefs. The social studies involves multiple perspectives and participatory citizenship that can be understood only through discussions.

Discussions can be planned and spontaneous. The key is to ask important questions that focus on the social studies topics and issues while probing the students' knowledge, drawing upon recall and rationale. You don't want your students to simply reiterate what you think they should know. You want your students to actually think and express their thoughts substantiated with a deeper comprehension and connections to their lives. Let's look at two different types of discussions both of which are important to incorporate into social studies instruction (Parker, 2006).

CONDUCT SEMINARS

Seminars usually begin with prior information read by students or presented to them as a video, tape recording, artifact, picture, speaker, and so forth. Generally the information or text is a primary source or a secondary source reflecting on the primary source; the text tends to be powerful, enlightening, and challenging. Discussions during seminars focus on the text exploring inquiries such as:

- What is happening in the passage?
- What is the event?
- Who is speaking?
- What is the individual or group saying?
- What is the message?
- Why is this message being communicated?

Seminar discussions delve into multiple perspectives and individual interpretations of the text. Students' comments easily build on other students' comments causing the seminar discussion to deepen and raise more questions than provide answers. Seminar discussions often culminate on a provocative note that lures students to continue their discussions and seek more information on their own. Think of a novel or movie that ends with you wanting to know more and discussing it with a friend at a book club or over lunch. These are the goals of an effective seminar discussion.

LEAD DELIBERATIONS

The second type of discussion is deliberation, an extension of the seminar. Rather than examining the text, deliberations explore questions such as:

- Why do you think the events happened?
- What does this mean to you?
- Have these events occurred in your life?
- How did the events make you feel?
- What is the best solution to this situation?
- What else could happen here?

The goal of deliberation is not just to reflect on the text, but to take action. The action could apply to one's individual life or the action could be one taken as a whole group. This shared decision making is exactly what you want your students to practice and learn in social studies. Anytime you can lead a deliberation moving away from the assigned text and facilitating a relevant conversation that leads to action, you have achieved the ultimate purpose of social studies.

In deliberation you want to:

- Take an honest inventory of what is occurring
- Check to see that the event or problem is shared
- Ask questions to explore conditions from many points of view
- Brainstorm all possible solutions and ramifications
- Allow alternative solutions to grow from deliberation
- Make a shared decision through consensus (to reach a solution everyone can accept)

Parker (2006) tells us that seminars and deliberations are essential to social studies classrooms as the seminar helps our students know more about the world through personal connections, and deliberation helps our students change the world so they take ownership and responsibility. The two kinds of discussion fit together and could be included in every major unit of learning. Knowing and doing summarize the importance of teaching social studies content and skills in ways that enlighten and empower all of your students.

ORGANIZE PROJECTS

Social studies presents the ideal time to develop all kinds of projects. The projects can be formal or informal, short-term or long-term, single-task or multi-task. You can assign projects to be completed individually, with partners, in small groups, or as a whole group. Projects can be highly academic or a combination of academic and social interaction. The projects can extend beyond the classroom into the school and community to include a service learning component. You can design a sense of community around the organization and completion of the project. Social studies is the perfect subject area for projects.

As you guide and direct projects, it is important for you to step forward to develop clear directions and provide the resources and supplies for students to be successful. Then you step back as students go to work. Your main role is to be the resource person guiding and facilitating the process for students who need help.

Box 5.2 has a list of ten project ideas, two each for civics, economics, history, and geography, and an integrated course delivery. These projects will connect your students to the community in which they live while learning in the classroom.

EXTEND LEARNING
BEYOND THE CLASSROOM

Social studies extends beyond the classroom, connecting students with the real world, especially their own neighborhoods and communities. You may achieve this through discussion on a daily basis, as a project during class, or as a culminating activity. Box 5.3 gives

---

Box 5.2   Ten Project Ideas and Their Primary Disciplines

1. Charting the changes in a topic related to rights and citizenship (civics)

2. Reading and preparing notes to debate a governmental issue (civics)

3. Diagramming the sources of income for the community (economics)

4. Comparing and contrasting the cost of trend items over time (economics)

5. Mapping the journeys of the early settlers in the community (geography)

6. Mapping one's own journey to the current location (geography)

7. Writing the history of the community (history)

8. Writing a personal family history (history)

9. Searching the Internet for various accounts related to a current event and preparing a presentation with visuals (integrated)

10. Reading a novel about a particular period in time, accounting for the civics, economics, geography, and history of the events (integrated)

---

ten strategies for strengthening connections beyond the class-room (and their primary social studies discipline).

LOOK FOR MORE IDEAS

We have just begun to skim the surface of the many ways you can expand your teaching repertoire. Keep these in mind as we now look at literacy, lesson planning, and collaborating with colleagues. We will return in Chapter 9 to discuss how to bring artifacts and outside resource people into the classroom as well as how to take your students on field trips and where you might go. Chapter 10 looks at how to use technology and the wealth of resources provided by the

---

Box 5.3 Ten Community Connections and Their Primary Disciplines

1. Observe a court in session (civics)

2. Job shadow community helpers (civics)

3. Talk to entrepreneurs on starting and/or running a business (economics)

4. Investigate an issue of global importance in the local community (economics)

5. Talk to a community developer regarding future projects (geography)

6. Experience a cultural excursion in the community (geography)

7. Collect an oral history (history)

8. Visit the local museum archives (history)

9. Conduct an environmental impact study (integrated)

10. Organize and implement a service learning project (integrated)

Internet. Chapter 11 is filled with more projects and programs by subject area that provide students opportunities to demonstrate the socials studies skills presented here.

Follow Your Students' Interests and Energies . . .

The big idea from this chapter is to make the learning all about your students. We know you are eager to be in charge and lead the way. But the success of an effective leader is measured by the success of the followers. You will be much more successful as a leader and a teacher when you put your students in charge as a group and individually. They will learn how social studies encompasses both content and processes that are essential for learning all other subjects and in their daily lives. But, more immediately, they will discover that when social studies is all about them, it is rewarding and fun!

Suggested Activities

1. Identify an upcoming social studies topic or issue. Select one or two skills from each area of social studies to coordinate with the topic or issue.

2. Plan two different discussions, one that uses Seminar and one that uses Deliberation. Make note of the pros and cons for using each type of discussion and how you can improve these approaches.

3. Ask your students what kinds of projects they would like to design for the upcoming units of learning.

4. Talk with other social studies teachers about their current community projects to see if there is one you and your students could either join or extend as your own project.

CHAPTER SIX

Develop Literacy to Build Social Studies Skills

As you guide your students through both the day-to-day activities and major assignments, you will build their literacy skills to comprehend and use social studies concepts and vocabulary. You must cover a huge amount of content quickly, and everyone's success will depend on your students' abilities to make important text connections. The secret is there are many ways to empower your students to interact and understand social studies effectively.

INTRODUCE LITERACY PROCESSES AND OUTCOMES

Literacy entails the whole experience of interacting with text through reading, writing, speaking, listening, and viewing. Literacy is both a process and an outcome where the participant is an observer, a consumer, a producer, and a critic. Fluency, articulation, communication, and expression are proficiencies set within a context for the participant to function responsibly, to feel ownership, and to take action. These qualities certainly pertain to understanding, applying, and appreciating social studies.

In social studies, the literate student can:

- Identify main ideas
- Sequence events
- Differentiate cause and effect
- Draw inferences and conclusions
- Distinguish fact from opinion
- Compare and contrast
- Elicit examples and nonexamples
- Recognize bias
- Interpret quantitative data accurately
- Ascertain frame of reference and point of view
- Explore multiple perspectives
- Make valid generalizations
- Defend a position
- Question a defense
- Anticipate outcomes

IDENTIFY VOCABULARY AND CONCEPTS

Social studies textbooks and documents are overflowing with new and precise vocabulary. It is important to select words and concepts that students will need to learn that will enable them to read text (Schmoker, 2006). These words should be practical, i.e., those that are commonly used and those that, though not common, will be found frequently in the study of social studies. Use the terms in context and with simply understood examples consistently and regularly.

> I like vocabulary. It enables you to learn new words, which relate to the things in the past. I also like how the book uses these words, so you can actually learn them and read them. Acting out, or drawing the words was something that one of my teachers did to make vocabulary exciting. It was fun, and I remembered the word, meaning, and what I drew/acted out.

> Jackie, age 15, Grade 10

As you introduce new words, pronounce them clearly and ask students to repeat them. Give a synonym or a brief definition. Have students complete a form or make vocabulary cards on which they also include a picture or a sample sentence using the new word. Finally, encourage students to use the new words.

Many teachers post and maintain a vocabulary list in the form of a "word wall" for support during silent reading and class activities. The visual display will reinforce the new learning especially if you use bold colors such as yellow, red, and black and you incorporate the display as a natural learning strategy during class.

From a new teacher: *"I discovered that some of my students enjoyed drawing and were happy to create "word walls" that listed new words and terms with identifying pictures. Instantly a new bulletin board was created! Students used the display as a reference point throughout the unit."*

We also suggest that you post and maintain a list of key concepts. Again, social studies concepts frequently are foreign and unique to your students. You probably are teaching the concepts within a particular context and you want your students to understand the concept within that context. Chapter 7 will discuss concepts and topics by subject area and in general. One effective way to display the concepts is with graphic organizers. For example, if the concepts are related to chronological events, use a time line. If the concepts are related to parts of an organization, use fishbone organizers. If the people in a passage are related to one another, use a tree. Graphic organizers are ideal for structuring the reading in meaningful ways.

USE THE TEXTBOOK AS A TOOL

> *In the textbooks, I like that they have side notes on the pictures, because it really helps you understand what's going on. I also like that at the end of the chapter there are section reviews to help you study for a test.*

> Rachel, age 11, Grade 7

One significant source of literacy in the social studies classroom is the textbook. Today's social studies textbooks tend to be voluminous, cumbersome, and expensive. Most likely, the textbooks were selected prior to your arrival. In the future, you may have some choices about which textbooks you want to use or use most of the time. And, at some point in your career, you probably will be asked to evaluate textbooks as new series are considered for adoption. A list of criteria to consider when evaluating textbooks can be found in Resource A.

Regardless of your thoughts and feelings about textbooks, you are expected to use them. Take time to know each one and to use it proficiently. The school has invested huge amounts of money in purchasing books for every student. Your students' parents also expect you to use the textbooks, and many parents want to see the textbooks at home once in a while, if not every evening. Some parents want to help their children and expect the textbook to travel back and forth on a daily basis if classroom sets are not also provided. Follow your department policy in assigning textbooks.

Many students cannot read the textbooks comfortably, and just the sight of the social studies textbooks upsets some students. Not only do the textbooks appear overwhelming, many students have experienced social studies teachers who did not know how to use the textbooks effectively with their students. It is essential for you to keep the reading assignments developmentally appropriate and reasonably manageable. Consider the average reading abilities of the students enrolled in each course you teach. Read the selection yourself and note the time required to read the selection slowly and carefully. Now add ten minutes. This will be closer to the length of time your students will need to read the selection superficially. You will need to add more time if you want them to read it meticulously.

Begin by acquainting all students with the special features of each chapter. Review headings and subheadings, how new words are introduced, how graphics are included to help explain text, and the guiding questions found either throughout the text or at the end of a passage. From a veteran teacher: *"I start each unit by 'walking' through the chapter in the textbook with the students. We read the captions aloud and discuss the pictures. I try to motivate them by recording their questions to make connections when we get to that part of the unit."*

Some students need additional support. For struggling readers and English language learners, shelter your instruction. The SIOP (Sheltered Instruction Observation Protocol) Model (Echevarria, Vogt, & Short, 2005) consists of eight components. The Preparation component, for example, suggests planning lessons carefully by selecting language objectives along with content objectives, supplementary materials, and meaningful activities to create context for learning.

The SIOP Model emphasizes adapting the textbook by rewriting selections of the text that cover the key concepts (with topic sentence and supportive details) to give to students. Additionally, the SIOP Model encourages keeping a few copies of the text set aside in which you add notes in the margins or add notes on overhead transparencies to summarize a page or handout that fits around the text. Reserve texts in which you have highlighted the main idea, significant vocabulary, key concepts, and summary statements for students to read first. Building background, using comprehensible language, and modeling expectations are other important features in working with English learners as well as other students.

GIVE STUDENTS A PURPOSE FOR READING

Always give your students a purpose for reading a selected passage. This is one of the most important strategies you can implement to improve reading participation and comprehension. Giving students a reason to read helps students identify and understand concepts or big ideas, vocabulary, relationships within the text, connections outside of the text with both the reader and world, and ways to manipulate new information for future investigations such as conversations and writing (Carmine & Carmine, 2004).

The purpose may be posed as a question. Importantly, the question should be clear, simple, and straightforward so your students can find the answer. You can ask higher-order and more complex questions later. The opening question also should be contextualized in that you provide a place, time, and some details. Perhaps your question connects with prior readings and class discussions. You definitely want the question to connect to today's world.

Here is an example: "Your assignment is to read pages 15–25 to find how 'wants' and 'needs' are the same and different. As you read, think about your own kinds of wants and needs." The reason may be posed as a quest for information for an activity or project. Continuing our example: "As you read, record your responses on a Venn diagram labeled 'Wants or Needs or Both.'"

Try to avoid using the questions at the end of the chapter in the textbook for the homework assignments too much or too often. You certainly are encouraged to read and to ask students to respond to the questions; generally there are many other great questions for your students to answer to comprehend the textbook. However, answering questions in the textbook should not become the means to the end. You can use one of the questions to give your students a reason to read. Or, you can use the questions as a model if your assignment is for students to write one question that the selected reading passage brings to their minds.

From a teacher: *"I select a couple of questions from the end of the chapter to have the students pose to each other as review or closure questions. This encourages students to pay attention to the questions as they read the assignment."*

If you are using chapter tests produced by the textbook company, you will want to review the questions at the end of the chapters and in your teacher's manuals to be sure that you have covered all of the corresponding material and vocabulary. However, we want you to construct meaningful and engaging learning experiences that allow your students to learn social studies in ways other than reading the chapter, answering the questions at the end of the chapter, turning in the answers to you, taking notes from your lecture, and taking the textbook company generated test. There is so much more to effective social studies teaching and learning!

START WITH READING ANTICIPATION GUIDES

To connect your students with reading their text and all other documents, start with some anticipation guides outside the textbook (Readence, Bean, & Baldwin, 1998). You may use these tasks as your lesson openers. Anticipation activities may be completed individually, with partners, in small groups, or as a whole group. These are your decisions to make. Table 6.1 has ten examples of anticipation guides. In each example, you provide the students with a different type of activity.

If you are allowing your students time to read a selected passage for the first time in class, you cannot expect all of your students to either complete the reading or to glean all you want for them to glean from it. Some students will be distracted and unable to concentrate fully. You should try all you can to reduce and eliminate distractions. However, some students simply cannot focus on their reading for even short periods of time. Consider recording the passages ahead of time and having those students listen to them as much as they can, using earphones with the text in front of them.

Table 6.1   Ten Reading Guide Activities for Social Studies Text

Given . . .	Students will . . .
1. A list of ten vocabulary words with two columns labeled *Know* or *Do Not Know*	Mark the ones they know and write a synonym or give an example.
2. Some key concepts with columns labeled *Agree* and *Do Not Agree*	Mark the column for each item; students may also give a rationale.
3. A diagram of a process that may or may not be correct with boxed numbers at significant steps	Mark the boxed numbers as *True* or *False*.
4. A graphic organizer with columns labeled *Before, During,* and *After* and a list of items	Place the items in the appropriate column.
5. A map and directions	Mark specified locations of places and lines as either *I think it is Correct* or *I think it is Not Correct*.
6. A statement stem that may be a fact or an opinion	Link the statement stem to their own perspective or that of someone in the text.
7. A topic or issue	Write two questions about the upcoming reading assignment.
8. A concept map	List all the possible extensions related to a particular event.
9. A series of continuums	Identify how much they either agree or disagree with a series of statements.
10. Some sentence starters	Predict possible outcomes.

You may want to assign your students to read a selected passage outside of class, i.e., during a study hall or at home, to be discussed the next day. In this situation, you will want to give your students one to two minutes to review the reading at the start of the discussion. Again, state your reason for reading to initiate a lively conversation.

FACILITATE READING RESPONSE STRATEGIES

Reading responses are used by students during and after reading. Reading responses may relate to the same sheet as the anticipation guide correlating the information acquired during the reading or in a different place. Responses may be kept as a journal entry, or on a poster, a graphic organizer, an overhead transparency, and so forth. Box 6.1 has ten examples of reading responses.

Box 6.1   Reading Responses for Social Studies

1. Reflect a position in a political cartoon.

2. Create a map reflecting change in political boundaries.

3. Draw a time line annotating events during the course of an election.

4. Recap a summary using vocabulary and concepts as a news account.

5. Develop a list of questions as a police investigation.

6. Construct a perspective from a particular point of view in a letter.

7. Promote an issue or agenda in a speech.

8. Organize vocabulary words and key concepts in a graphic organizer.

9. Write a response and pass it to a partner or group member for a comment.

10. Identify bias in a political position statement.

INCLUDE ALL KINDS OF TEXT

In addition to your textbook, there are many kinds of text useful for teaching your social studies curriculum. Some are primary sources and some are secondary sources.

Primary sources are original items from the past and documents written by individuals who provide information about their own direct experiences during an event. They include speeches, letters, diaries, and oral histories as well as their photographs and other personal belongings.

Secondary sources are documents written by individuals who have researched information and offer an interpretation or analysis based on primary resources. Secondary sources include history books, journals, magazines, and encyclopedias.

Table 6.2 has a list that we urge you to investigate:

Help students differentiate between primary and secondary sources and the purposes for each one. Explain the importance of citing their sources and model the process of writing a citation. As there are different citation styles, be sure to let them know which one(s) they should follow.

Table 6.2   Different Types of Social Studies Texts

atlases	faxes	routes and times for airplanes
biographies	graphs	schedules
calendars	instructions	signs and posters
captions	journals	speeches
charts	laws	street and road signs
computer data	letters	telephone directories
constitutions	magazines	television guides
court records	manuals	thesauruses
diaries	maps	timetables for buses and trains
dictionaries	menus	trade books and novels
documents	newspapers	travel books and brochures
e-mail messages	poems and songs	treaties
encyclopedias	recipes	visas
essays	reports	weather maps

INTEGRATE VARIOUS TYPES OF WRITING

Literacy involves not only all kinds of text, it also involves all types of writing. Many literacy experts (Strong, 2006; Zinsser, 1988) purport that students better understand what they read when they write as they are visibly and authentically engaged in their learning. They personalize their knowledge. Daily or weekly quick writes or journal entries provide students with records of what they have learned. They may want to reference this work as they study for tests or create a project/presentation.

We can believe that students are actively engaged in their learning when someone is talking and they are listening. However, you cannot be sure of what is actually happening. When your students are writing, they tend to listen more attentively to what is being said by you and others. As they process information, they tend to select more precisely what they are recording. They use critical thinking skills. During the writing process, students realize that teachers and peers can or will see what they are producing. And most of your students want to look good in front of their peers, possibly more than they want to look good for you.

When students are writing in social studies, you want them to:

- Use social studies vocabulary and concepts correctly; this means contextualizing the meanings accurately and precisely
- Transfer the vocabulary and concepts correctly to new and different contexts either literally or figuratively
- Construct their own uses of vocabulary and concepts to new and different contexts and applications to advance their thinking

Writing can be expressed in ways that include:

- *Expository*—Conveys information or explains what is difficult to understand; i.e., documents, summaries, news reports, magazine articles
- *Narrative*—Tells a personal story or fictional experience based on real or imaginary events, i.e., autobiographical incidents, eyewitness accounts, historical fiction, plays
- *Persuasive*—Attempts to convince the reader to accept a particular point of view or to take a specific action; i.e., focused

analyses, advertising campaigns, political speeches, newspaper editorials, social criticism

- *Technical*—Relates scientific information or principles; i.e., evaluations, instructions, directions, hypotheses, formal arguments, problem solving

Table 6.3 suggests different types of writing exercises.

GRANT YOUR STUDENTS WRITING P.O.W.E.R.

To teach writing skills, use **P.O.W.E.R.** (Street, 2002). This writing process involves five steps to empower students in expressing their ideas on paper. Students begin with **P**rewriting (brainstorming thoughts), such as freewriting, asking questions, talking, listening, and reading. Then comes the task of **O**rganizing (meeting a purpose).

Table 6.3   Different Types of Social Studies Writing Exercises

autobiography	interview
advertising campaign	journal entry
biography	letter
brochure	magazine article
contract	mission statement
diary	newspaper article
editorial	obituary
essay	play
evaluation	political speech
eyewitness account	report
graphic organizer	speech
historical fiction	social criticism
hypothesis	treaty

Next, students engage in **W**riting (capturing ideas), followed by **E**scaping (taking a break). Finally students turn to **R**ewriting (polishing the work). Teachers serve as coaches to support students in their efforts as they find power in writing.

TRY THE DRAFT WRITING PROCESS

Another creative way to engage and empower students in the writing is to use **DRAFT** (Gallavan, 1997). DRAFT is a strategy where students **D**esign a written piece that allows them to write from a unique and personalized perspective. Students select the **R**ole of the writer, the **A**udience that will be reading or hearing the writing, the **F**ormat of the writing, and the **T**opic. For example, students can assume the **R**ole of a newspaper editor, address the **A**udience of newspaper readers and citizens in general, write in the **F**ormat of a persuasive editorial, and discuss the **T**opic of immigration.

Example of DRAFT: *Students can **D**esign a diary and take the **R**ole of the border between Mexico and the Southwestern United States. The **A**udience is both border crossers and border guards. The **F**ormat is a diary entry reporting the events of the day. The **T**opic is immigration from the perspective of the inanimate object that sees all that happens.*

Take time to brainstorm a variety of DRAFT ideas with your students so they can select the writing combinations that suit them.

DEVELOP OBSERVATION SKILLS

Whether working with objects or photographs, students need to develop observation skills. Teach appropriate vocabulary related to the object, the photography, and/or the time period. Ask students to objectively describe what they see, then share their subjective reactions to it. Have students consider who produced the item, when it was made, the purpose, and reception by various groups of people. With photographs, discuss what or who might be missing and whether it is a posed or candid shot, the composition of the picture, what might have happened before and after. Adapt the following form to your purpose. Figure 6.1 is a sample Viewing Guide Form.

Figure 6.1 Viewing Guide Form

Observation Form*

Item and Reference	Historical Perspective	Physical Description	Personal Reaction	Questions
Date, creator	What context it relates to . . .	What it looks like, including color, texture, pattern . . .	How it makes you feel . . .	What you wonder about . . .

Teachers and students should expand this form as needed.

REFERENCE CURRENT EVENTS

Your students will enjoy their social studies class much more if you can make the curriculum relevant to their everyday lives. Using current events and controversial issues exemplifies authentic application of the five qualities of powerful social studies teaching and learning as well as the skills of literacy. Plus there are many visual aids. Pictures, graphs, charts, and maps provide effective visual references to support student learning. Newspapers, magazines, and television programs often present bulleted summary points to guide understanding. Students make immediate connections.

Find present-day occurrences that are interesting and meaningful to your students. Perhaps there is a new construction or transportation project being considered for development. How will that impact their lives? Look for current events in the school and local newspapers to share in class and to post on the bulletin board. A veteran teacher shares: "I use Time for Kids *to teach current events. This type of magazine is a good source of information and models reading throughout life.*"

Use current events as the context when introducing and reinforcing concepts. From another teacher *"I use* Newsweek *magazine to update the textbook.* Newsweek *enables students to put faces with names like Condoleezza Rice and John Roberts. Most teens have a small sphere of a world, and the nightly newscast has no place there. Like all things academic, most of them whine and complain to start, but cultivate an appreciation for brand new issues each week and are sad when their subscription ends. Often students will continue personal home subscriptions after we are finished in class."*

Some schools use the "Newspaper in Education" program (for which there is now an online resource http://nieonline.com) with a political cartoon section, lesson plans, quizzes, and other resources. Other schools use student newspapers or student magazines targeted at grade and reading levels. Look in your subject area for related publications.

> *My favorite way to study current events is to have class discussions and friendly debates. This enables you to learn more about the event and learn classmates' views on what is happening in our world.*
>
> Laura, age 15, Grade 10

ADDRESS CONTROVERSIAL ISSUES

Introduce controversial issues too. You will capture your students' attention immediately once you tell them some of the arguments surrounding the lesson (Hess, 2005). Students are attracted to learning about controversial issues once they discover the learning is not fixed as in traditional learning. Many different ideas and possibilities suddenly abound when delving into controversial issues.

Examining controversial issues incorporates multidisciplinary and interdisciplinary approaches to teaching and learning as they replicate real life events that your students encounter in their lives outside of school and at home. Part of the democratic experience is to disagree. We all benefit from organized opportunities to learn how to listen, sort information, pick our position, and defend it with sensibility and sensitivity. Teaching and learning about controversial issues is exactly what social studies is all about.

Either you alone or with your students can select controversial topics and issues to investigate and discuss. We suggest that you always maintain the right and responsibility to decide and clearly communicate the expectations with your students. You want to be careful that students do not have an agenda that they are attempting to convey within the confines of your social studies class. The topics and issues may be of interest internationally, nationally, and locally, as well as representative of individuals or groups.

When using controversial issues in your social studies classes, be sure to:

- Allow enough time to select, delve, and discuss them
- Involve all of the students fairly and equitably
- Provide access to plenty of information and resources
- Explore multiple perspectives and opinions
- Connect the learning with standards and content to illustrate big ideas and to advance social studies knowledge, skills, and dispositions
- Model sensitivity if (and when) the discussion becomes heated and uncomfortable for some students or misrepresents you and the school
- Maintain dignified control to reroute or end the discussion if necessary
- Allow time for closure and debriefing that may lead to alternative outcomes and social action

You may find your district has specific guidelines for discussing controversial issues. There may be a list of topics you are not allowed to discuss in class or with students, formally or informally. Though students may confront you with questions or statements, you will need to explain your district's policy. In one school district that we know, teachers were not allowed to present controversial issues; however, students were allowed to raise and then discuss such issues. Teachers carefully try to address all points of view, and presentations need to be suitable for the age and development of their students. If you are caught off guard by a turn in conversation, discuss with students the need for preparation and return to the topic another day. For extremely sensitive issues, you may want to inform and consult with your appropriate administrator.

Hess (2005) reminds teachers to be aware of their own political views and how their words and actions can influence students easily. She identifies four approaches teachers commonly take: (1) denying that an issue is controversial and there is one correct position; (2) teaching toward a particular perspective; (3) avoiding the issue because of strong feelings; and (4) promoting a balanced approach that considers various positions. Effective teachers realize that their own positions influence their decisions.

Using current events and controversial issues makes the learning active and fun. Information is examined critically and in-depth in ways that the students find authentic, purposeful, and relevant to their lives. Students are motivated to access additional resources and are fascinated to learn new and different perspectives. It prepares them for future political participation. These are some of those wonderful teaching moments in social studies where teachers overhear their students saying, "I didn't know that. . . . "

In the next chapter we look at how to develop a lesson plan with instructional strategies to engage students. We will share specific ideas for selecting themes and concepts, opening and closing your lessons, and guiding in-class activities, and out-of-class assignments successfully. Your class will be one that students look forward to each day.

Equip Your Students to Learn Independently . . .

Social studies skills prepare your students to interact on their own as participants, consumers, producers, and critics of social studies knowledge. Teachers rely heavily on learners' levels of literacy and their abilities to read, write, and view images objectively and from multiple perspectives. Integrating literacy and social studies helps prepare your students as lifelong learners. Therefore, effective teachers will integrate literacy development as they build social studies skills.

Suggested Activities

1. Reflect on your interactions with social studies textbooks. Which features will you want students to use?

2. List three forms of text that inform and support your social studies knowledge. Discuss how you will share these with students.

3. List three types of writing that express your social studies knowledge. Which types will you integrate in your classroom?

4. Investigate your district's policy on controversial issues. Discuss experiences with a colleague.

CHAPTER SEVEN

Plan With Students in Mind
to Prepare Your Teaching

The best approach to use when planning your social studies curriculum, instruction, and assessments is to imagine how your students view coming to school, learning in general, and learning social studies specifically. Unfortunately, many students simply do not like social studies. They think it is a dead subject about people, places, and events from long ago and far away that has nothing to do with them. Your challenge is to develop your curricular content, design your instructional practices, and align your authentic assessments so the learning is captivating and meaningful in ways that connect with your students' lives here and now.

SELECT YOUR UNITS OF LEARNING

Let's begin with the big picture. Most of you will be responsible for creating and implementing your own units of learning that you develop for your particular style of teaching and your particular group of students. After you are assigned your courses and the grade levels, we suggest that you concentrate on the curriculum; lay out the state standards, keep the school district expectations handy, and open the textbooks. Now think about your students' interests as well as your own energies.

Many of you will follow the chapters as they are presented in the textbook. By doing this, the chapters in the textbook most likely will determine your units of learning. You may think you are compelled to follow this plan as many social studies books, especially history books, are organized as a giant time line starting long ago and continuing toward today. Also, information and vocabulary in the second chapter tend to build upon the first chapter and so on throughout the book. Perhaps you will be more confident if you adhere to this plan during your first few years of teaching.

However, you have choices. You can teach the textbook chapters in your own order, supplement them with other materials, or reorganize the material to fit your own curriculum design. For example, some history teachers like to start with the most recent chapter and work backward through time. They say that this approach captures their students' interests immediately as the information is more current and relevant to their students' lives. Plus starting with the most current chapter can establish the means for a valuable dialogue between students and their parents and grandparents at the start of a social studies course and new school year.

For other social studies courses, teachers may select the order of their units and thus the order of their textbook chapters. Here's a helpful secret. By talking with the other social studies teachers at your school, you can learn more about how they organize their units of learning. You may also find you have joined a department where the teachers follow a pacing guide, and benchmark tests are administered on a set schedule. Or, in some schools resources have to be shared and teachers rotate the materials and units they teach. In this situation you will need to collaborate with the other teachers. You may find you will not have as much freedom as you would like to have in making curricular planning decisions.

HIGHLIGHT CONCEPTS

All of your units will include specific concepts (McCarthy, 1997). Usually the state standards and school district expectations include an extensive list of important concepts. Concepts are single words or short phrases that represent high-level, abstract ideas or beliefs key to their academic discipline; concepts symbolize large bodies of knowledge and reference a hierarchy of knowledge that increases and decreases by generality, complexity, and abstractness (Taba, 1962). See Table 7.1 for sample concepts by subject area. In Resource B you will find an extensive list of social studies concepts.

EMPHASIZE SIGNIFICANT THEMES

Teach the concepts by emphasizing the significant themes related to your subject area (Manning, Manning, & Long, 1994). Themes connect the concepts or big ideas that address essential understandings with social studies standards and academic expectations mentioned in Chapter 2. Themes can be dissected through assorted approaches and viewed from multiple perspectives. Rather than presenting information passively, invite students to explore significant themes to involve them in their own learning processes. To fully understand a theme, students will rely on previous learning in this subject area, and they will also utilize concepts and practices learned in other subject areas. Table 7.1 presents examples of themes linked to concepts by subject area.

TEACH DOMINANT TOPICS AND ISSUES

Next, take a look at the dominant topics and relevant issues connected to the concepts, and construct lists to reference throughout the school year. These lists of topics and issues become the outlines of your units of learning. Most social studies teachers have identified ten to twenty main topics and issues to guide their units of learning during a school semester.

Concepts and themes give your students a context for understanding the topics and issues. Students examine many different ideas and issues that impact their lives now as well as in the future. They become more active and engaged in the learning when the learning is relevant.

Table 7.1 provides a chart of how all these elements align. You will see examples of concepts, themes, topics, and issues with

Table 7.1 Chart of Sample Concepts, Themes, Topics, Issues, and Examples

Subject Areas	Concepts	Themes	Topics	Issues	Examples
CIVICS	citizenship	rights responsibilities	laws voting	requirements	*age *gender *property *race *registration *taxes
ECONOMICS	capitalism	patterns changes	savings investments	options	*bank accounts *land *property *stock portfolios
GEOGRAPHY	weather	natural disasters	relief specific conditions	preparation	*cyclones *hurricanes *tornadoes *tsunamis *typhoons
HISTORY	recreation	changes over time	games toys	national origins	*board games *construction activities *dolls *stuffed animals *wooden toys
GENERAL SOCIAL STUDIES	respect	free speech	newspapers magazines	truth	*cartoons *editorials *election endorsements *letters

examples related to civics, economics, geography, history, and general social studies.

After you identify the concepts, themes, topics, and issues, then specify your objectives and reading passages to isolate the vocabulary and thinking skills. These items will help you organize your learning experiences, incorporate various forms of expression, balance assignments throughout the unit, and select alternative assessments. All the while you want to break the learning into manageable pieces for students to master. Box 7.1 contains a list of the factors in planning a unit.

From a veteran teacher: *"I start planning the instruction by selecting pictures from historical eras and geographic locations to give students a visual reference. Then I choose which primary documents I will have students reference so they have the opportunity to look at many different types by the end of the year. Finally, I determine the types of activities to provide a variety of experiences."*

Box 7.1   Checklist of Factors in Unit Planning

_____ Social Studies Course and Grade Level

_____ State Standards

_____ School District Expectations

_____ School Mission

_____ Students' Special Interests

_____ Concepts

_____ Themes—NCSS Thematic Strands

_____ Topics and Issues

_____ Texts and Other Resources

_____ Educational Goals and Objectives

_____ Vocabulary and Thinking Skills

_____ Learning Experiences and Forms of Expression

_____ Assignments

_____ Assessments and Evaluation

ENVISION YOUR PLANNING SCHEMA

Many teachers like to develop patterns for their units. By developing schema or a specific and consistent approach for planning your units (Yildirim, 2003), you and your students will feel comfortable, participate more easily, and enjoy the teaching and learning readily. Setting a pattern will help the students have a sense of order when, for example, they can anticipate how much they are expected to read for each unit, how many assignments they have to complete on their own and with others, how many presentations they are expected to make (again on their own and with others), and how they will be assessed.

Let's start with a sample unit schema where each unit is taught for fifteen days. (See Figure 7.1.) Other units may be planned for a week. (See Figure 7.2.) Regardless of the time, you must consider how each day will be allocated to achieve your goals and the students' objectives. This type of schema helps students plan their lives and take control. You, your students, and their parents will appreciate this approach.

Figure 7.1   Three-Week Unit Blueprint

Each day select some type of reading response mechanism to give your students a reason to read and an opportunity to react to the reading.

Day 1: Introduce unit; preview vocabulary and concepts; use textbook as resource; assess prior knowledge	Day 2: Connect with current events, personal experiences, and common artifacts	Day 3: Reinforce the vocabulary and concepts; make unit assignments	Day 4: Show video segment to demonstrate application of topics and issues in the real world; return previous assessment, discuss progress	Day 5: Revisit unmastered topics and issues; conduct an in-class activity
Day 6: Debrief class activity; assign groups; prepare for guest speaker	Day 7: Listen to guest speaker presentation	Day 8: Access Internet and/or library resources	Day 9: Work on group presentation	Day 10: Finalize group presentation preparations
Day 11: Share group presentations	Day 12: Share group presentations	Day 13: Review group presentations, topics, and issues	Day 14: Review unit assessment	Day 15: Assess unit

Figure 7.2   One-Week Unit Blueprint

Give a reading assignment for homework the first three days and a writing assignment as review for homework on the fourth day.

Day 1:	Day 2:	Day 3:	Day 4:	Day 5:
Introduce unit; preview vocabulary and concepts; textbook as resource	Connect with current events, personal experiences, and common artifacts; add additional content	Reinforce the vocabulary; add additional concepts; conduct class activity	Show video segment to demonstrate application of topics and issues in the real world; jigsaw cooperative groups	Review vocabulary and concepts; assess learning

You want to plan your entire unit of learning as far in advance as possible and with as much detail as feasible. This process helps you to attend to all parts of the unit, look at it from multiple perspectives, locate resources, and make special arrangements with plenty of time to ensure that one unit of learning flows seamlessly with the previous unit and into the next unit that matches your students' energy levels. From a middle school teacher: *"I like to let students in groups choose how they will demonstrate what they have learned. I present them with the eight multiple intelligences and have them select which one they will use for a presentation to the class. Students then look forward to a variety of presentations, from songs to posters to interpretive dance and other demonstrations of skills, knowledge, and dispositions."*

FOLLOW A CONSISTENT LESSON PLAN FORMAT

Preparing a lesson plan will give you a specific roadmap to follow once the class period begins. On the plan you will list your standards and objectives. You can anticipate the order of events from a "warm-up task," to introducing the lesson, to activities, to closure. Then, you will identify instructional adaptations and modifications for specific students and your assessments. Finally, you will indicate what your closure activity will be. You can anticipate your homework assignments and include any announcements. Listing the resources you need for the lesson will enable you to quickly gather any special supplies you will need for a given period. Using a consistent lesson plan format will help ensure that you have thought out all parts of your lessons. A detailed lesson plan format is found in Resource C, and an abbreviated lesson plan format is found in Resource D. The sections below present suggestions for the various sections of a daily lesson.

UNDERSTAND ATTENTION SPAN

Most likely, you can hold your students' attention in one activity for approximately 30 minutes and probably less with younger and less mature learners. Today's students are conditioned to a limited amount of concentration, a heightened sense of immediacy, and a reduced level of self-sufficiency due partially to their habits with television and movies, computer games and the Internet, e-mail, and cell phones. You are a part of this generation too, only now you are the teacher, and you can channel these habits into effective social studies teaching and learning.

In a traditional class period, your class can be subdivided into three main time segments to facilitate effective teaching and learning opportunities: (1) opening the learning; (2) leading students through the body of the lesson, such as facilitating in-class activities or guiding projects; and (3) closing the learning. You will select different types of strategies to fit each of the time segments. In this chapter we describe ten strategies to exemplify each time segment. You may discover that some of the examples listed in one time segment can be modified and used in a different way. We strongly encourage you to find more strategies and add them to your repertoire as your social studies teaching career develops.

> *Class activities are much better than sitting in a desk reading a book. I enjoy playing games and making posters. These activities help you better understand the material.*
>
> Olga, age 14, Grade 9

CAPTIVATE STUDENTS AS YOU OPEN LESSONS

The first time segment involves opening the learning process so that you can grab your students' attention immediately and completely. When students arrive, make sure you have set up the classroom specifically for that group of students by arranging desks, organizing teaching strategies, and preparing learning activities. You might want to follow an established daily routine, or you might want to introduce something different every day or every few days. There are many different models of teaching (Joyce & Weil, 1996). Whatever approach you prefer, you will want to set the stage for the entire class period. Consider the following ten easy-to-implement activities.

Ten Opening Activities

1. *Hand a prompt:* Greet students at the door, and hand them a paper or other item related to the upcoming learning experience. Instructions can be written on paper or posted on a board or screen.

   a. Hand all of your students the same item, such as copies of a question to answer or a problem to solve in the first few minutes of class. Students can work independently, with partners, or in small groups.

   b. Hand your students different items such as puzzle pieces to form a huge puzzle assembled by the entire class or papers of different colors to be used in small groups.

2. *Post a prompt:* Post information on the board or a screen with an overhead. Ask a question, give directions, or pose a problem related to the posted prompt for students to complete individually, with partners, or in small groups. The prompts may

   a. reflect the reading, listening, or viewing;

   b. connect topics and issues with the real world;

   c. survey current beliefs and behaviors;

   d. ask for predictions and/or suggestions.

3. *Display an artifact* (or a mystery item): Place an artifact in a highly visible location and ask students to discuss the item. Or you can display a mystery item and have students make guesses based on some clues or answers to their questions. You can conduct this opener individually, with partners, or in small groups, as an oral or written response.

   a. Have students name the item, describe the item, or guess what the item is as statements.

   b. Have students pose questions that enhance their critical thinking.

4. *Show a video clip or take a virtual Internet tour:* Show a few minutes from a video, computer program, or Internet connection.

  a. Have students describe what they have seen, and discuss observations in either small groups or the entire class.

  b. Have students express their feelings connected with the viewed selection or predict how the viewed selection related to a particular topic or issue.

5. *Play a recording:* Start playing a recording while students are entering the classroom. The recording may be music, a speech, a poem, instructions, and so forth.

  a. Have students report what the recording makes them think and how the recording makes them feel.

  b. Have students follow the instructions on the recording.

6. *Read aloud:* Start the class by reading a selection aloud. The selection may be any kind of narrative used in many different ways.

  a. Have students report what the reading makes them think and how the reading makes them feel.

  b. Have students write a similar piece individually or in small groups.

7. *Introduce a guest speaker:* After students are settled, introduce a guest speaker. The speaker's visit may be planned, and students may have constructed questions in advance. Or the speaker's visit may be a surprise.

  a. If the speaker's visit is planned, have students take a few minutes to write down and discuss what they know about the topic.

  b. If the speaker's visit is a surprise, give students a few minutes to record some questions before the speaker talks.

8. *Silent reading:* Instruct students to read a passage silently for the first five to ten minutes of class and provide a reason for reading, preferably written on a paper, the board, chart, or an overhead transparency. The passage may be from the textbook or any supplementary materials, particularly primary documents.

  a. Have students respond to the reason.

  b. List key vocabulary words and concepts from the passage and have students describe the concepts using vocabulary.

9. *Brainstorm ideas or make a guess:* Show a chart or poster displaying a scene, data, cartoon, and so forth.

  a. Have students brainstorm or guess what is happening in the scene or the purpose of the data.

  b. Have students write questions they could ask, or identify investigations they could take to find out more information.

10. *Play a game:* Games used to start class could feature activities that can be played without direction. Games can be used in previewing upcoming learning, scaffolding or revising prior learning, reviewing or applying new learning, or preparing for assessments. When using games as an opener, be sure to

  a. distribute all necessary materials in advance;

  b. follow previously established rules;

  c. limit to the first ten minutes of class;

  d. connect the purpose of the game with upcoming learning.

BEGIN THE LEARNING EXPERIENCE

If you spend the first ten minutes for the class opener, you have approximately thirty-five minutes remaining for the body of the lesson, with five minutes left for closure and five for any administrative tasks (announcements, clean up.)

You want to move into the learning experience quickly and smoothly. If your students figure out that you can be distracted or drawn off the subject, most likely it will occur at this time. Be aware that your students will know exactly when and how to start unrelated conversations to delay the start of your planned lesson.

After assessing your students' prior knowledge or schema, you want to identify the starting point of your teaching and their learning. If gaps are identified, you can build new knowledge by introducing additional experiences and visual references. You have two distinctly different paths to follow: *indirect teaching* or *direct teaching.*

START WITH SOME DIRECT TEACHING

If you follow the direct teaching path, information is given to your students either by you, via lecture and example, through shared reading, or through another medium, via video or guest speaker(s). Direct teaching allows you to cover a huge amount of content quickly and with control of the pacing, engagement, and expectations. It is essential that teachers begin by stating the objective for learning and providing graphic organizers for students to take notes and make connections. Direct teaching certainly plays an important role in social studies classes.

Most teachers rely primarily on talking with students formally and informally to provide information. These personal conversations also provide feedback attributing to your assessments of students' understanding and achievement. Effective teacher talk (Callahan, Clark, & Kellough, 1998) both encourages and requires students to listen in a way that constitutes active engagement in the learning process.

Guidelines for Direct Teaching

• Outline your talk to have a beginning, middle, and end, with a logical order of information and events that provides background or extends rather than repeats what is in the text.

• Provide an outline or study guide, preferably in the form of a graphic organizer, for students to follow your talk, take notes, and make connections (Ausubel, 1963).

• Use visual aids, such as illustrations and artifacts, slides, transparencies, charts, drawings, videos, realia, physical demonstrations, and so forth.

• Incorporate vocabulary, concepts, and examples naturally within the body of your talk.

• Apply familiar examples to connect the learning with your students' prior knowledge and experiences.

• Consider diversity in the content and examples.

• Use notes to guide your talk; be sure you speak to and *not* read to your students unless you are reading explicit directions that must be followed precisely.

• Encourage participation with and among your students.

- Monitor your voice quality (tone and volume) and eye contact.

- Move around the classroom and speak from various locations; this technique helps make all students feel included in the conversation and forces students to stay alert.

- Reinforce key ideas and significant outcomes with closure.

Direct teaching includes expository and demonstration teaching. *Expository teaching* provides an explanation using facts, ideas, and other vital information to transmit basic knowledge and essential skills specified by the curriculum. Table 7.2 shows the structure of expository teaching describing the teacher's role, the student's role, and nature of assessment.

Demonstration teaching involves showing, telling, and/or conducting performances relating knowledge, skills, and dispositions through efforts and endeavors that may be planned or spontaneous frequently combined with the modes of exposition and inquiry. Table 7.3 shows the structure of demonstration teaching.

Both types of teaching are often used in a given lesson. Here is an example in World History. Using *expository teaching*, you might discuss significant events in history occurring in different places during a given period. Students would take notes and then be assessed with a quiz or essay. Using *demonstration teaching*, you would model for students how to create an annotated time line of events. Students would observe what you do and then create their own time lines, which you would assess. Both knowledge and skills are involved in this unit. Teachers choose their methods to achieve their objectives.

Table 7. 2   Structure of Expository Teaching

Teacher's Role	To direct the learning, primarily through teacher talk and media presentations
Student's Role	To listen, to record notes
Assessment	Based on recalling and reproducing correct answers of a predetermined curriculum

Table 7.3   Structure of Demonstration Teaching

Teacher's Role	To plan, organize, and execute the demonstration clearly
Student's Role	To observe, listen, and follow the presentation carefully
Assessment	Based on the ability to participate, replicate skills, or respond to questions and discussion during or following the demonstration

FEATURE INDIRECT TEACHING

The indirect teaching path engages your students in their own learning. The teacher becomes a facilitator of learning, guiding with questions and providing resources. There are several steps to follow with indirect teaching.

Guidelines for Indirect Teaching

- Introduce the activity. You can give an overview and all the details at once, or you can give an overview and inspect each detail one at a time.

- Provide reading response mechanisms. Most activities conducted in class will relate to the textbook; you and your students will benefit from guided reading response strategies and reviewing the text features. Some options are listed in Chapter 6.

- Monitor student progress, keeping an eye on the time. Allow plenty of time. Students may be slow in getting started. Be prepared for the activity to grow and change as students get involved and take ownership of their own learning and outcomes. As you interact with students, give fair, frequent, and positive feedback for participation.

- Collect products with students' names on them at the end of the activity to use during upcoming class sessions, to give feedback, and to record their participation in your grade book.

There are many different types of indirect activities for you to try with your students (Hoge, et al., 2004). The amount of time and kinds of materials that are needed vary with each teacher, group of students, and course content. Student grouping is another factor to consider. Indirect teaching allows for *differentiated learning* as students address objectives with a variety of activities and resources. The presentations that result give you and the students a wonderful opportunity to share their learning with others, i.e., students in other grade levels, parents, and the community.

Ten Indirect Learning Activities

1. *Inquiry*—Stimulate students to develop questions when investigating new events or building on prior knowledge and experiences resulting in description (telling what it is), significance (telling how it is relevant), and justification (telling why it is relevant) (Costa, 1991).

Inquiry-based or problem-based learning uses immediate problems as the foundation of study. The teacher may select a topic or have students participate in the selection of a problem to be solved. Students may work as a class or in small groups to define the problem, research the background, propose various solutions, and then pick the best solution for presentation. Having an authentic problem and audience makes these experiences especially meaningful. Students learn how to work together and how to solve problems as well as master the issue or topic under study.

2. *Data Analysis*—Introduce topics and issues substantiated with research-based information and statistics along with narrative descriptions of situations and incidents (quantitative and qualitative data). Have students examine cause and effects, trace interconnections, consider multiple perspectives, and evaluate implications related to concrete and abstract, real and fictitious conditions and events.

3. *Discovery*—Facilitate learning experiences by placing students in new situations where they can observe, react, question, describe, compare, contrast, explain, and interpret events in their own terms and through their own means (Brunner, 1959; Taba, 1962). Tell students they are detectives responsible for determining

what they know, what they need to know, what they do not need to know, what others may or may not know, and so forth. The popularity of detective television programs supports this activity.

4. *Critical Thinking*—Develop learning experiences that challenge students and cause them to wonder, doubt, and question the given situation or status quo (Beyer, 1995). Ask students to consider a topic or issue from a different perspective, a viewpoint they probably would never take on their own to research and defend to a group through a presentation, debate, or staged event, such as a trial.

5. *Concept Attainment*—Formulate significant ideas for students to comprehend, explain, apply, and appreciate both simple and complex issues generalized or transferred from meaning and experience (Parker, 2005). Concepts are big ideas that tend to be somewhat difficult for students to realize and apply to new or different contexts. Introduce and reinforce concepts slowly and deliberately with many explicit examples for complete attainment.

6. *Cooperative Learning*—Organize students to function in small groups where they draw from one another's wisdom and strengths to understand given information, to construct new knowledge, and to teach themselves and others (Johnson & Johnson, 1989). We strongly recommend that you teach your students cooperative learning techniques early during the school year using a relatively easy concept so your students fully understand the roles, responsibilities, and rationale of cooperative learning. Then, after some practices and debriefing the group process, you can use cooperative learning activities as a technique that your students can apply readily to more complex concepts and skills.

7. *Role Play and Simulation*—Have students role play historical or current events. They can simulate real procedures, such as in moot courts, and evaluate real policies, such as in town meetings or legislative hearings, as they demonstrate their knowledge, skills, and dispositions. Students practice skills in the classroom that they will be able to use in real life. They conduct research and present their findings. Simulations help students develop social justice and critical thinking skills.

Simulations seem to work best when teachers have participated in the simulation themselves and a careful debriefing takes place following the interaction (Singleton, 2006). This way the teacher is fully aware of what learning takes place, the length of time, the kinds of materials, and the type of setting needed, and the level of stress experienced if the simulation is presented in front of an audience. Clearly explained objectives and directions are critical for success using simulations. A follow-up discussion is equally important to give students the opportunity to summarize and clarify what they gained from the experience, to what degree their thinking changed, how well they worked with others, and how the simulation relates to real life.

8. *Debate*—Select an age-appropriate, relevant topic for your students about which ample reference material is available. Present the debating procedures to the students. They need to understand the roles played by participants, the impact of the rules, and how the debate will be judged. Then, students need time to research, write, and practice their delivery. What better way for students to distinguish fact from opinion and explore different points of view? What better way to integrate listening, speaking, and literacy skills in the classroom? You can even consider engaging students in a different location in a debate using technology (Hess, 2004).

9. *Project-Based Learning*—Design long-term, interdisciplinary, student-centered, collaborative learning experiences for students to take stock of current situations and accepted norms and then propose viable solutions integrated with real world issues and practices (Evans, Newmann, & Saxe, 1996). Project-based learning requires several steps that you want to develop completely before starting them with your students. Usually the steps involve reading, writing, inquiry, interviewing, field trips, drawing, technology, and presenting. Think of project-based learning as a real life event that adults have to commonly perform around their homes or at their work. Students attach themselves quickly to project-based learning as they can apply their personal touches to the outcomes.

10. *WebQuests*—Take students on a virtual "quest" for information to answer a question, solve a mystery, create a product, or other predetermined task. Bernie Dodge with the help of Tom March developed the model of inquiry-based research on the Web in 1995 at San Diego State University. WebQuests provide students with specific directions and Web links so as not to have them spend needless time searching for information. They take one to three class periods or longer.

Select a WebQuest your students will find interesting and provide some background information. Then, give the directions for completing the task, including resources and organizational tools to be used. Use an assessment rubric for guidance. At the end, have students present and summarize their learning.

Teachers have found great success in assigning students to groups or teams for WebQuest activities. With time and experience, students can create their own Web Inquiry Projects (WIPs) that are open-ended tasks with limited teacher scaffolding. In WIPs, students select their own data to analyze and present to their peers. A good reference for reading and educational materials can be found at http://webquest.sdsu.edu where Bernie Dodge also maintains a free Web site with 2,500 examples for Webquests and http://edweb.sdsu.edu/wip for WIPs (Molebash & Dodge, 2003).

REINFORCE LEARNING DURING CLOSURE

Just as you wanted to motivate learners when you opened the lesson, now you want to reinforce the learning during closure. Too often, closure is simply the ringing of the bell followed by the closing of books. We recommend that you leave the last five to eight minutes of class to bring the learning to a close. By capturing the most important points and relating them back to your objectives you enable your students to process what they have learned. By having students record their findings, the learning will be strengthened. Box 7.2 shows a variety of ideas for closure.

PLAN HOMEWORK

You will need to consult the homework policies for your school district, school building, and teaching team. There may be clear guidelines as to the frequency, the amount, and the types of homework that you can and cannot ask your students to complete.

Homework assignments need to have clear purposes related to your social studies topics and issues. Students must be able to complete the work on their own and communicate expectations with their parents. Homework is the perfect opportunity to include families and to make meaningful connections outside of

Box 7.2   Ten Closing Activities

1. Write one statement, question, comment, or connection on a note card.

2. Make a daily entry in a journal.

3. Record information on a graphic organizer.

4. Summarize facts or beliefs on a group paper or poster.

5. Vote on a preference or prediction.

6. Take a stand on an issue.

7. Ask a question of a partner.

8. Make a connection and share with a group.

9. Write a summary with each member of the group adding a sentence.

10. Construct a quick quiz question for everyone else in the group to answer.

the classroom. For example, you may ask students to interview a parent, grandparent, or neighbor to find out more about a particular historical event.

With homework, you can vary the types of assignments you want your students to experience given the limited time in the classroom. Homework can build upon individual learning styles and serve as conduits for students to share personal interests. Sometimes, you may be able to give students a choice of assignments.

While typical assignments involve reading and studying notes, some types of homework assignments are new tasks given to students to complete explicitly outside of the classroom and, perhaps, specifically at their homes. The homework assignment may be a written product or a presentation preparation that students complete outside of the class using the library, Internet, or other resources. Each of these types of assignments may be difficult, if not impossible, for all students to complete if the students are not given appropriate access and supplies, time, or opportunities are not available to them outside of school. In these situations, alternative assignments should be offered. Check with your students to make sure each student is capable of achieving success.

From a veteran teacher: *"The more time I spend planning my lesson, the smoother the delivery will be and the more time students will be on task. Homework has students apply what they've learned, gives an opportunity to practice new vocabulary, concepts and skills, or prepare (a reading assignment) for the next day. By carefully planning for each lesson, we all experience success in meeting standards."*

Make the Most of Your Time . . .

Ideas are endless, but time is limited. Be aware of the time as you teach your classes knowing exactly when to start and stop each activity, moving through the opening, guiding the lesson activities, and closing each day. The secret is to make the most of your time in the classroom and your students' time outside of the classroom. Try new strategies. Evaluate to see which ones are best for your students. In the next chapter we will explore how to collaborate with colleagues to expand your students' experiences and enrich their learning.

Suggested Activities

1. Plan a lesson from introduction to closure using both formats in the Resource section of this book. Discuss the advantages and disadvantages of each.

2. Make a large chart with the segments of a typical class and use sticky notes to start designing your teaching strategies for your units of learning.

3. Observe teachers to see how they implement and transition through the parts of a lesson plan. Discuss with a colleague.

4. Ask your students to give you feedback on their favorite learning experiences.

CHAPTER EIGHT

Collaborate With Colleagues to Expand Opportunities

"*I have been so lucky. I have always worked with a great team of teachers. Even after twenty years of teaching, I am amazed how much I learn from my colleagues and how much I depend on them to keep me going every day. Teaching social studies these days is challenging: The textbooks are hard for students to read, the tests are overwhelming, the parents are not much help, and the students aren't ready. I can talk with my team members to commiserate and to get ideas; they give me nonstop support. I like it that we can teach and laugh together.*"

This reflection summarizes one social studies teacher's experiences about collaborating with her colleagues. As a middle school teacher, this teacher teams with four other teachers in her grade level. This teacher also works closely with two other social studies teachers at her grade level, as well as all of the teachers in the middle school social studies department. These three layers of organization empower the teacher in knowing her students and understanding their school day holistically; aligning her social studies plans and preparing her activities with teachers assigned the same courses; and interacting with social studies professionals and exchanging ideas to stay current in the field. Your organization structures and functions will be similar. We will describe what you can anticipate and the secrets to negotiating these layers to ensure your success.

EXAMINE COLLABORATIVE APPROACHES AND PRACTICES

Effective collaboration gives teachers a mechanism for working with a collection of diverse individuals who share interests and energies. Hopefully, everyone on your team likes teaching, the subject areas, and the age group of the students. Cooperation and creativity work together to satisfy the academic expectations and to generate new ideas. You can integrate your curriculum, instruction, and assessments in many different ways to meet the needs and interests of the teachers, students, and school (Fine, 1995). Together, you can plan, teach, and evaluate your teaching and your students.

We suggest you keep these key approaches and practices in mind.

1. Combine team members wisely considering subject areas and individual teaching styles.

2. Establish teachers' teaming expectations regarding the outcomes and processes.

3. Determine members' responsibilities for all tasks, including planning meetings, facilitating discussions, taking notes, distributing minutes, attending to details, reporting to administrators and other teachers, serving on committees, monitoring progress, and so forth.

4. Identify expectations for the students, including management, rewards, and consequences that are positive, fair, and consistent.

5. Stay focused during meetings; arrive prepared to maintain positive and productive professionalism.

6. Recognize and appreciate the knowledge and skills in others as strengths; build upon the diversity to expand

your own viewpoints and the educational experiences you are providing for your students.

7. Share resources, materials, ideas, responsibilities, recognition, and rewards.

8. Coordinate activities, projects, and events.

9. Hold meetings with your students frequently to communicate team expectations.

10. Celebrate achievements.

ADOPT THE SECRETS OF SUCCESSFUL COLLABORATORS

Collaboration must be based on important personal attributes held by each individual and shared mutually. The secrets to success are to adopt qualities of professionalism. (See Box 8.1)

Box 8.1   Qualities of Professionalism

trustworthiness	humor	enthusiasm
respect	patience	commitment
flexibility	risk-taking	resiliency
openness	responsibility	resourcefulness

Then teachers can organize and operate with shared purposes and risk-taking related to teaching, learning, and schooling. Teachers, especially new teachers, need frequent chances to ask questions, articulate concerns, and contribute openly and honestly with receptive faculty, staff, and administrators. All teachers need opportunities to reflect. Collaboration requires an optimistic sense of adventure that, if conducted professionally, will serve you and your students well.

CONSIDER VARIOUS TEAMING CONFIGURATIONS

There are various configurations for organizing teaching teams. Each configuration engages teachers and students in different scenarios to fulfill different outcomes. Some teaming configurations are permanent and some are temporary. There are advantages and disadvantages to these configurations so weigh your options carefully (Alleman & Brophy, 1993). Here are some teaming configurations for you to consider and try:

1. *Team Planning*—Team teachers exchange ideas and coordinate events collectively but teach individually; teachers are responsible for their own classrooms but align their school agendas and share student concerns at a weekly team teachers' meeting. Usually, four or five teachers serve on the same team and teach the same grade level; team members may or may not teach the same subjects as one another. We suggest you (a) keep notes in a notebook to reference throughout the year and during future years, (b) select a team leader as the team coordinator and liaison, and (c) distribute responsibilities equitably.

2. *Teaming with Departmentalization*—This configuration is the same as number 1 above but teachers share the same students. Usually four or five teachers serve on the same team and teach the same grade level while students move among all the classes. The team consists of one teacher per subject area of language arts, math, science, social studies, and maybe reading, library, foreign language, or technology. Again, we urge you to keep notes, to select a leader, and to distribute tasks.

3. *Teaming with a Shared Resource Center*—This is the same as either number 1 or 2 above, and the team shares a resource center such as a specialized library, media center, or technology lab. In some schools, these types of resource centers are located in the center of the area or pod and are supplied with tables, chairs, and assistants. Teachers can use the resource center with students during instructional time, or teachers can arrange to send students individually or in groups to access the services available in the center.

4. *Single Teacher Planning*—One teacher plans and prepares for all other teachers on the team who follow the stipulated instructional plan; this configuration tends to happen only on occasion to

fulfill a specific purpose or when one teacher is an expert in a particular subject. The teacher gets everything ready and all the other teachers teach according to the plan using the provided materials. For example, the social studies teacher writes a lesson plan about voting, collects the materials, and equips the three other team teachers to teach the same lesson on a national election day.

5. *Identical Teaching Across the Team*—This is the same as number 4 above; however, all teachers on the team help with preparation and teach the same learning experience in each classroom, with all members of the team contributing parts of the planning, instruction, and evaluation. For example, all four teachers show the same video about weather emergencies and safety procedures, ask their students to write and practice informative skits in small groups, and prepare to make presentations for the entire team. This learning experience would require literacy, math, science, and social studies as well as fine arts, research, and technology.

6. *Integrated Instruction Across the Team*—Like number 4 above, this configuration requires all team members to teach an aspect of the same curriculum. In this situation, students rotate among the team teachers to learn various aspects of an overarching theme, topic, or issue. For example, the social studies teacher plans and organizes four different lessons related to changes over time with transportation in U.S. history, with each teacher focusing on a different time era.

7. *Traditional Team Teaching*—Two teachers work together; each prepares and teaches one entire group of students two different aspects of one theme, topic, or issue. The teachers may teach the same subject area or different subject areas. For example, with two social studies teachers, one teaches the map skills and the other one teaches the cultural dynamics. With a social studies and language arts teacher, the social studies teacher leads students through an exercise in conflict management and the language arts teacher guides students through a related exercise in expository writing. The nonteaching teacher assists the teaching teacher by writing instructions or samples on the board, providing and/or monitoring student progress, and so forth. Both teachers remain in the classroom and actively engaged with the instruction.

8. *Collaborative Team Teaching*—This configuration is a modification of the traditional configuration by involving two teachers

in the teaching and learning at the same time. For example, the two teachers introduce the fishbowl discussion strategy to explore issues related to urbanization and the environment. Both teachers contribute in giving students directions and both teachers participate in the activity. This teaming configuration requires the two teachers to be equally knowledgeable with the concepts and practices as well as comfortable with an interactive teaching style.

9. *Supportive Team Teaching*—This looks like number 8 above with one teacher guiding the initial or direct instruction for the two groups of students then the other teacher providing follow-up practice. The team could be two social studies teachers or two teachers from different subject areas. For example, the first social studies teacher introduces the concept of needs and wants; the second teacher guides in-class activities to apply the concept to personal contexts.

10. *Parallel Team Instruction*—Two teachers and two groups of students work together in one space; each teacher leads one group of students through the same instruction. Students form one large group and share outcomes at the end of the learning experience.

11. *Differentiated Teaming*—Like number 10 above, groups are divided according to specific purposes: abilities, interests, learning styles, needs, and so forth. Each teacher leads instruction to one group; the instruction in each group might be similar but the content or practices will be unique to the needs of the group. The teaching team can decide if outcomes will be shared as a whole group or within groups as a culmination.

12. *Monitoring Teaming*—Similar to numbers 8 through 11 above, one teacher guides two groups of students combined in one setting throughout the entire learning experience and the other teacher monitors students' progress and manages behaviors by moving among the students and providing individual intervention. For example, the social studies teacher models how to label a U.S. map with the states, capitals, mountains, and rivers. The second teacher circulates among students to prompt and assist as necessary.

We want to emphasize that you can create and combine all kinds of teaming situations throughout the school year to serve many different academic purposes and social outcomes. The variety will captivate your students' interests and help keep your teaching fresh and alive.

KNOW PROS AND CONS OF TEAM TEACHING

There are many advantages as well as disadvantages to team teaching that we want to share with you now before you leap into making an uninformed decision. We know that some of you will have no choice whether you team teach or not. This decision may have already been made before you arrived or you interviewed at a school where team teaching is the norm.

Some of the advantages of team teaching include:

- Teachers specializing in their subject area, providing expertise where the content is more complex
- Teachers consolidating the materials and resources into one space and being ready to teach all related curriculum in that subject area
- Teachers getting to know their students extremely well in that one subject area
- Teachers teaching what they enjoy and expressing their passion with their students
- Students being grouped together by abilities or interests, allowing teachers to focus on particular content and skills in ways that are developmentally appropriate to differentiate instruction more efficiently
- Students being more attentive to and engaged in learning since they travel through their day with the same group of students (or most of the same students), following the same schedule
- Special service teachers working with identified students who are grouped together within the team
- Teachers working together more efficiently and effectively to plan their lessons to meet the needs and interests of their students
- Students learning one daily routine that increases their success
- Teachers conferencing with students and parents more efficiently to discuss the student's progress holistically

Conversely, some of the disadvantages of team teaching include:

- Students communicating more fully with one teacher than the other teacher(s)
- Students cooperating more with one teacher than with the other teacher(s)
- Students not completing homework equally for all teachers
- Students "playing" one teacher against another to get their way just as children "play" their parents against each other
- Students who are "tracked" labeling themselves as more advanced or less advanced than the other tracks
- One class elevating itself above the others as a teacher's favorite
- Students being challenged to stay organized and ready with materials; materials tend to be left in lockers or other classrooms so students interrupt both the class they are in and the class where materials have been left when they have to retrieve their missing items
- Students being challenged to stay organized and finish their homework; it is helpful to have one homework assignment sheet for students to record their assignments throughout the day to show their homeroom teacher at the start and end of each day and to share with parents at home at night
- Teachers not liking the teaming assignments, the decision-making model, or some (or all) members of the team. Personality conflicts may arise within a team that can be detected by the faculty, students, and the students' parents. It is beneficial to establish a standing meeting time, place, and procedure with one person assigned as leader to manage the group.
- Teachers needing to be prepared for working as a team and making collaborative decisions. Administrators should review the process at the opening of each school year and highlight what works and what doesn't work. Wise administrators will meet regularly with team leaders to improve communication, productivity, and document progress. They will rotate team leadership so all teachers learn how to be effective leaders and followers.

UNDERSTAND SCHOOL ORGANIZATIONAL PATTERNS

Most likely your teaming configuration(s) align with your school's organizational patterns. School schedules may be organized around various lengths of time such as the entire school year, two semesters, three trimesters, four quarters, or other time segments for year-round schools. Your social studies classes may be scheduled to meet every day at the same time for the same length of time.

Or your social studies classes may be scheduled in a block to meet every other day at the same time for a longer period of time. In this organizational pattern, students attend the same number of classes each day, but classes meet on alternating or scheduled days. Your team configuration may be limited to the same teachers who share the same daily schedules with you and your students.

You may be assigned to team with one or more other teachers with whom you share a block of time. For example, you and the language arts teacher may be assigned one hundred minutes and two groups of students. You and the language arts teacher must decide (a) how to divide the time, (b) how to divide the students, and (c) how to align your curriculum, instruction, and assessments. Look over the list of team teaching configurations; we think you will find one approach that fits your needs and interests.

MAKE THE MOST OF DEPARTMENTALIZATION

Many of you will work primarily with the teachers in your social studies department. Most often you will plan, teach, and evaluate with your grade level and meet occasionally with other social studies teachers. For the most part, your courses will be taught independently of the other courses on your grade level team except for some culminating projects and shared school events. Here are some advantages or strengths related to departmentalization:

1. Students will be taught by teachers who specialize in their subject areas.

2. Teachers can focus and concentrate more on their own subject areas.

3. Teachers can develop overarching plans for only a few courses and can individualize instruction for students in various sections of the courses as needed.

4. Departments can identify major outcomes and assign them or aspects of them to various teachers to assure coverage, sequence learning, and avoid redundancy.

5. Departments can expand and enrich learning or even provide multiple perspectives related to a select topic or issue; teachers can explore complex issues from conflicting points of view.

6. Teachers can organize and allocate time and energy for integrated culminating projects and school-wide events.

7. Students experience unique yet coordinated learning styles and situations.

8. Students learn to make transitions quickly and smoothly, particularly if only a few transitions are expected of younger or less mature learners.

INTEGRATE SOCIAL STUDIES ACROSS THE CURRICULUM

The knowledge, skills, and dispositions of social studies play a huge role in relationship to all other middle level and high school subject areas. Since social studies examines learning about people throughout time, in all places, and from different points of view and circumstances, no other subject area can be taught or learned without integrating social studies. You could say that social studies is the glue that holds all other subject areas together.

For example, when the math teacher introduces a mathematical formula to explain how numbers relate to one another, the math teacher most likely illustrates the situation with a real life application. We call these applications word problems where students must read the problems, apply critical thinking skills to comprehend the questions, generate the appropriate mathematical formulas, and solve the equations. Mathematical word problems instantly become social studies as they present real life circumstances involving people, time, and places.

One teacher told us with laughter in her voice: "*Everyone cringes at the age-old math problem that begins: 'Two trains from opposite directions were approaching each other on different tracks . . .' Thinking mathematically, we want to know the speed of the trains and their distance apart. However, thinking through the social studies lens, we want to know what kind of trains they are (steam, electric, bullet . . .), the terrain of the land (flat, mountainous, curvy . . .), the location (urban, open country, tunnels . . .), and what they are transporting (people, food, nuclear waste . . .). From the social studies perspective, we suddenly want to know much more of the story behind the math problem. These issues play a huge role when solving this math problem in real life.*"

The same thinking certainly fits with the teaching and learning of science. Topics and issues of science readily involve beliefs and attitudes too. Once people get involved with questions of science, the subject becomes social studies. For example, when discussing the environment or natural resources and land use, many social studies questions must be explored. The different scenarios or outcomes impact people far and wide, now and forever. These outcomes constitute the knowledge, skills, and dispositions of social studies.

Let's turn to the subject of English, especially literature. When one is reading either fiction or nonfiction, the context of the text selection instantly involves social studies as the reader connects with the people, the time, the place, and the particular elements of the plot. In social studies terms, the reader is immersed in sociology, history, and geography along with politics, economics, law, and/or religion. Clearly, all the circumstances embedded in literature connect with the knowledge, skills, and dispositions defined by social studies.

> *Last year, I did a puppet show about the Louisiana Purchase. It was a fun experience because we got to make a script, which helped us really understand what went on during that time. We also got to make our own puppets, and perform our show. Then we got to watch everyone else's shows about different events in that time, relating to ours.*
>
> Kiera, age 16, Grade 11

Working with other subject areas to reinforce common academic vocabulary will support student acquisition of new words and terms. The repetition will strengthen students' ownership as they see the relevance of this vocabulary across disciplines.

In summary, the stronger a student's understanding, application, and appreciation of social studies becomes, the more successful the student will be at understanding math, science, English, and the elective courses. And consequently, students will be more proficient, demonstrating mastery through papers, projects, and tests as well as in social settings, such as group work, academic clubs, and civic organizations involving critical thinking, problem solving, and decision making both at school and in life.

To integrate social studies effectively, lay out the standards and expectations for two or more subject areas. Connect the standards that fit together naturally. For example, if you are teaching social studies and language arts, use the language arts standards and expectations to guide your reading and writing responses to the social studies themes and topics. Students can collaboratively conduct a research study on a contemporary issue or become involved in a service learning project.

From a curriculum specialist: *"One of the most successful projects I have seen is called Earthquake! In eighth grade geography, students study earthquakes and their effects while in their corresponding English courses, they read informational texts and work on writing skills to develop reports and posters. The English learners benefit by seeing the same vocabulary in both classes in a rich print environment. These teachers integrated technology, too! The students and teachers were proud of their accomplishments."*

Integrating art lessons can be another way to successfully collaborate. Students often say the most fun activities are the art projects. Plus, the art teachers often have needed supplies!

> *We made masks. They were supposed to be Egyptian. Each person's mask was of their face. Their partner covered their face with Vaseline and then applied plaster strips. After it was dry a few days later, we got to paint it and decorate it like an Egyptian's would have been.*
>
> Maria, age 12, Grade 8

If you are the social studies teacher working with one other teacher, share your standards and resources to help everyone focus on some in-class activities and culminating projects. Students can develop portfolios of outcomes informed and supported by standards from different subject areas to be shared at parent-teacher conferences.

USE BLOCK SCHEDULING WISELY

Block scheduling, in which students have ninety minutes or more for a class period, are great settings for social studies. Students have longer amounts of uninterrupted time for research, discussion, and presentation. Teachers can easily combine elements of direct teaching and indirect teaching during one class session. Students can engage in one major concentrated learning experience or a variety of activities during one period. There is plenty of time for guest speakers. You can revisit content in a multitude of ways.

Managing block scheduling periods effectively requires you to be well prepared with plans, materials, and patience. You need to know exactly what you expect to happen throughout the entire block. Both you and your students will find your energies fluctuating, so it is important to give explicit instructions along with appropriate time limits to complete activities. Then be alert to when it is time to end one set of activities and switch to different activities. Most students are not able to sustain their attention for ninety minutes on a single assignment. Either you will want to start and stop the entire class at regular intervals to monitor progress and comprehension, or you will need to meet with groups during the block to check on your students.

Team teachers can work together to decide how students will spend the block time each day: all with one teacher, all with the other, or split in some fashion. Portions of time may be spent with both teachers. Block schedules offer great flexibility.

From a teacher: *"American Studies students cover U.S. history standards with me in their history class and then move on to their American literature teacher for the next period. We do our unit planning together. Sometimes we merge the classes for a large, group discussion. On simulation days, she may allot a portion of her time for my students to complete an exercise; on writing days, I give her more time. Flexibility and patience definitely are required."*

TALK TO TECHNOLOGY SPECIALISTS

Teachers who are interested and advanced in technology or who have become specialists will be a great asset to you. They can help you design creative experiences for students and keep you up-to-date on the latest technology developments. Ask them to model how they use tools, such as the graphing calculator (already used in science and math) to represent numerical data from field investigations or digital cameras to record history.

Many schools are now encouraging teachers to develop their own Web pages as resources for students and parents. You can post assignments and rubrics, homework help, reading schedules, special events, and test dates. Additionally, you can post supplementary material and Web links for extended research. Once you have gained permission, you can display pictures of your classroom and special activities that take place there. Perhaps, you'd like to create podcasts of lessons for students who are absent or for students to review before taking a test. You will find it helpful to contact your Information Technology department for directions and guidance.

Classroom computers and/or videoconferencing systems will allow you to communicate with people outside the classroom. You can conduct interviews with resource people, job shadow professionals in the field, or collect survey information. As students receive information, they can create databases to record and organize their results. With the help of specialists you will be able to provide a technology rich classroom and stay abreast of legal and ethical issues.

CONTACT OTHER EMPLOYEES IN THE DISTRICT

There are likely several resource people available at your school or in your district who will be able to make contributions to your curriculum. They can serve as guest speakers on a variety of topics for your students. The school resources officers or local police officers can come and speak about the importance of laws in our society and enforcement for a civics or government class. Perhaps the school psychologists will talk about human development or the effects of stress on the body for a psychology class. School counselors can talk about group processes in a sociology class. School social workers might alert students to community agencies in your area for a health class.

With a little time you will discover who has come to teaching as a second or third career. These individuals can provide your students with a personal look at the role of a business owner, a military officer, or a Peace Corps worker. They will share their experiences living and working in the U.S. and abroad in a variety of capacities. Many teachers will talk about their personal histories, such as the times they lived and the corresponding events and issues that impacted their lives. The teachers in your school are resources too; if you offer to take their classes for a day, they will be able to be guest speakers for yours. Having guest speakers increases the sense of immediacy and personalizes the learning for your students.

SEE SOCIAL STUDIES IN SOCIETY AND THE WORLD

Help your students see social studies in society and the world by exploring state, regional, national, and international dynamics. You might be amazed to find businesses and agencies in your neighborhood that operate nationally and/or internationally. Consider the connections to your curriculum.

When looking at social studies in society and the world, we suggest you use maps, newspapers, television, movies, sports, and the Internet. Making global connections is a fabulous start for integrating the curriculum that you and your students will find captivating and rewarding.

Finally, you can join with others to celebrate International Youth Day, which promotes the ways in which young people contribute to their societies. The United Nations has established a different theme every year since 2000. You can have your students participate in discussions that focus on youth issues. Or plan programs that showcase their achievements. See www.un.org/esa/socdev/unyin/iyouthday .htm for more information.

Integrate Social Studies Naturally . . .

When you integrate social studies with another subject area, across your team, or throughout your school, you have achieved the ultimate goal. You want your students to experience social studies holistically, naturally, and authentically in their learning. You plan their activities and projects to be filled with inquiry, curiosity, exploration, discovery, application, and appreciation. You want them to connect the standards and outcomes with their everyday lives and future endeavors. In our next two chapters we look at a wide variety of resources to support your efforts in making social studies come alive.

Suggested Activities

1. Talk with an experienced social studies teacher about teaming pros and cons.

2. Work with a partner to plan an integrated unit. Decide what content you will incorporate. Identify the specific objectives to be covered and the assessments to be implemented.

3. Connect social studies with a schoolwide event such as a curriculum fair by collaborating with other teachers to integrate learning outcomes and presentations. You and your colleagues can design a menu of possible presentations styles such as poster sessions, research papers, and dramatic demonstrations.

4. Explore opportunities for involvement in parent-teacher organizations.

CHAPTER NINE

Incorporate Resources *to Make Social Studies Real*

T opics and issues will leap off the written page when you and your students bring a variety of resources to class to share with one another. When your students can see and touch items from an actual event or hear someone who was there talk about their first-hand experiences, focus of learning shifts. Instead of being on the outside looking in passively, now you and your students are inside taking an active role in the learning process. Expanding the textbook concepts and standard practices with reality establishes context for your students to make connections and to build community.

Your students can ask meaningful questions that are relevant to both the social studies unit of learning and to their own lives. They link significant concepts to their own experiences and stories they have heard in their families. You strengthen your communities of learners when they openly share their thoughts and feelings. Incorporating resources into your social studies classes will greatly increase your students' interest in social studies and enhance their academic achievement through powerful teaching and learning (Farris, 2005).

SET THE STAGE

There are many different types of resources and many different ways of using them in your classes. It is essential that you are well prepared and plan far in advance. It helps to arrange or reserve many of the resources as early in the school year as possible. Therefore, it is important to be extremely organized and forward thinking as you order materials to be sent to your school, invite guests, coordinate field trips, and so on. For loaned or rented materials you may have little leeway with the time and get to keep them for a few days. However, with most outside resources, you will generally have only one day to use them. Here is a guide to follow as you get started.

Resource Planning Guide

- Identify all of your units of learning for the entire school year with the approximate amounts of time you want to allocate for each one.
- Check all of the applicable calendars, such as activities, substitute availability, testing dates, and so forth to avoid schedule conflicts.
- Share your plans with your department head, social studies department members, and team members to add their suggestions.
- Brainstorm three to five types of resources that would enhance each of your units of learning; perhaps you can brainstorm with a colleague.
- Inquire about the resources available in your media center and school district; there may be many resources right at your fingertips.
- Talk with your library/media specialists who may have already coordinated resources pertinent to your anticipated units of learning in the past.
- Acquire some heavy cardboard boxes or large plastic crates, along with colorful files for each anticipated unit of learning, to collect and organize your own collections of resources.
- Develop a filing system of folders or a three-ring notebook divided into your anticipated units of learning for each course you will be teaching; record your unit ideas and the

contacts in each subdivision of the notebook. If you record your plans and contacts on your computer and other electronic organizers, be sure to make a hard copy to keep in your file or notebook. You may want to carry the information with you when you go to the telephone, when you visit off-site resources, and go home.

The secrets to using resources are to know your subject, your audience, and your purpose. As you select resources, especially when inviting guest speakers and taking field trips, your time and energy will be efficient, effective, and appreciated by your students.

INTRODUCE ARTIFACTS AND REALIA

Social studies concepts and practices will make much more sense when you bring in the actual objects or models representative of the objects that you are describing. These objects and models are called *realia* and are vital to effective social studies. For example, if you are studying international currencies, you can bring in real money from around the world. You will have to go to a bank that exchanges money. Tell them that you are a teacher, and they may exchange it for free. Perhaps you want to exchange money for coins only and get pictures of the larger denominations from either the bank or the Internet to share with your students. You can keep the coins in enclosable plastic bags and the pictures in your files in your boxes or crates and store them for the next year.

Once you show your students the realia or memorabilia that you bring to class, your students will want to bring their realia and memorabilia too. Continuing with our example, some students may have traveled out of the United States. They may have samples of international money at their homes. Invite your students to bring their realia to school. You might want to send a note home to parents or via e-mail to let them know what you are studying and how students can get involved. With younger students we suggest that you ask students to bring the money to you first thing after they arrive at school for you to keep. Have a box of enclosable plastic bags and some markers handy so you can write the name of the student and amount of money brought to school. You should take responsibility for the realia brought from home. Ask your students if you can share the realia in your other classes. With our example of money, sharing would probably not pose any problems. However, you can ask your students to bring other kinds of realia from their homes, and you want to be sure you can share their personal objects with other students before doing so.

From a veteran teacher: "*Whenever I teach U.S. history I bring in a sample of a cotton plant when we read about plantation life in the South. Students are able to see the size of and feel the parts of the plant. The 'Ah hah!' experience takes place only when students are able to actually feel the seed in the bloom of the plant. It is then that they are able to understand the difficulty of separating the cotton from the seed. As they see the plant they are able to appreciate the extensive labor involved in picking cotton.*"

You can find all kinds of realia and memorabilia. Discuss with your students ahead of time not only how they are expected to treat the realia but also how they are expected to express their reactions. Some realia is old, rare, and fragile. Students should look at, but not touch these objects. Some realia is personal and perhaps controversial. Remind your students that the objects represent thoughts and feelings of individuals who have experienced many different aspects of life. We encourage you to engage your students in powerful learning activities to make connections to their own lives and to explore multiple perspectives.

From a veteran teacher: "*I have a set of white cotton gloves that I distribute to students before we look at items we need to handle with care. This makes the experience special and helps remind students that the objects are fragile. After the session, I collect the gloves, wash them, and put them away for the next experience.*"

Students' parents will have all kinds of realia and memorabilia to share too. Send a note home the first week of school previewing your upcoming units of learning and to ask parents if they would like to contribute or get involved by sharing their objects. You might be surprised at the extensive amount of realia parents have inherited from their families and acquired from developing personal collections. You can either invite the parents to be guest speakers and share their realia themselves in your class or classes or to send their objects and collections to you to share. If parents visit one of your classes and you are teaching several sections of the same social studies unit of learning, invite the parent to stay for the day. We suggest you provide lunch for the parent, take photographs, and be sure to write a note of appreciation following the visit.

FEATURE THE NCSS NOTABLE BOOKS

One of the best resources for you to use in your social studies classes either in place of or in addition to your textbooks are the National Council for the Social Studies' Notable Trade Books for Young People. Since 1972, a committee of educators who are members of the NCSS, in cooperation with individuals from the Children's Book Council (CBC), identify an extensive list of books that can be incorporated into all kinds of social studies classes. The selected books provide excellent resources for you to integrate literacy and social studies through contemporary fiction and nonfiction.

The books highlight human relations, diversity of groups, and a broad range of cultural experiences. Additionally, the books share original themes or new slants on traditional topics, can be read easily, offer high literary quality, and appear in a pleasing format with a variety of illustration formats, such as photographs, pictures, and so forth. The selected books are identified with one or more of the ten NCSS thematic strands as well as the recommended grade levels to help educators coordinate the texts with the curriculum. Lists of the annual NCSS Notable Books can be accessed at the NCSS Web site: www.socialstudies.org/resources/notable/. Here you will find current lists for members only, as well as past lists free of charge. We suggest you talk with your colleagues and librarian as you develop your units of learning. Perhaps you will want to start collecting some of the books and organize them with your units to have ready as you prepare your yearly plan.

ORDER EDUCATIONAL TRUNKS

Here's a wonderful secret we want to share with you. Many school districts have acquired or have access to educational trunks that are aligned with state standards and filled with all kinds of related artifacts, teaching ideas, and additional resources. You can even find trunks at various museums located across the country that can be sent to you. Universities also may have trunks for you to check out from resource centers or curriculum libraries. We have listed some additional sources in Chapter 10.

We suggest you order trunks early in the school year and coordinate your order with the other social studies teachers in your building. Many times, there are more items in the trunk than you can explore during one or two class sessions. The items can be integrated across the curriculum too.

When the educational trunk arrives, it is helpful to make a copy of the shipping order and take inventory of the items that have been included. We suggest you conduct the inventory on your own, taking time to inspect the items carefully for damage and to be sure they are there. As you look at the contents, you can start planning how to share them with your students. Note on your copy of the shipping order the items you remove from the trunk and share with your students during each class session or loan to another teacher. Then when it is time to return the trunk, conduct one final inventory to be sure all items have been packed properly in the trunk.

Educational trunks usually do not contain authentic realia since these items would be too valuable or impossible to replace if lost or broken. The trunks usually contain replicas and models that fully illustrate the concepts and practices. However, you want to show your students exactly how you expect them to inspect the objects, ask questions, glean information, form opinions, and make connections. See Chapter 6 for the Viewing Guide Form.

From a veteran teacher: "*One of the best educational trunks on Thailand I've seen is available from our university. It held not only the usual videos and posters of the people and countryside, coins, stamps, art, and fabric but also examples of children's toys, children's books, clothing, and musical instruments. The students could try on the clothes, play with the toys, and try the musical instruments.*"

Often trunks include teaching suggestions, such as a notebook of worksheets from which you can select and make copies for your students. Or, the trunks may include ideas for additional explorations you can conduct in your classroom, specifying items such as books or materials that you will need to acquire to teach the lessons. There may be a list of individuals you can contact via telephone or Internet to speak to students and videos you can show to your class.

INCLUDE VIDEO AND AUDIO SELECTIONS

Videos offer you and your students opportunities to see as well as to hear, or hear about, and to understand people, places, objects, and events that your textbook and discussions cannot communicate completely. You have many different video choices such as documentaries, reenactments, travelogues, and so forth. Whatever you choose, select only the portions that are relevant for your lesson.

After you determine that a particular video or DVD matches your standards and expectations, you need to decide the appropriate time in your unit of learning to show it. You can show it at the beginning of the unit to initiate interest and inquiry and to provide background knowledge. You can show it midway through the unit to introduce new information and to build upon prior learning. You can show it at the end of the unit as review and extension. Also, you can show it in your class and have team members integrate instruction. For example, you might show a National Geographic video about water. In social studies you connect it to rivers and environmental issues. In science, students relate it to natural resources and usage issues. In language arts, students use the video as the basis of a debate.

After deciding the purpose(s) and timing for showing a particular video, identify how you will guide your viewers before watching the video and how you will ask your learners to respond during and after watching the video. Take time to communicate your expectations for students' behaviors. If you are expecting your students to take notes, you have to provide lighting or know exactly when to stop the video for your students to write. Likewise, if you plan to stop for discussion, you need to know when to pause the video for such interaction. The goal is to create a seamless series of learning experiences throughout your unit with the video as just one more event.

There are many wonderful audio resources from speeches to music to enhance student learning too. Students will benefit from hearing original speeches recorded in audio format. Discuss the context for the speech and the reactions that resulted at the time. You might want to provide a copy of the text for students to follow along with the recording to assist your visual learners.

Students also will enjoy hearing music from around the world and from different time periods. Use your music teachers as consultants. Students' attention spans are brief when asked only to listen, so it is important to play short, relevant pieces. When possible, provide words and/or a music score to guide them. Show pictures of the composers, musicians, and instruments as visual aids.

There are several items to consider in determining the suitability of any media selection.

Media Previewing Questions

- Length: Can you show/play the piece or selected segment during one class session?
- Content: Does the media address main ideas essential to your theme, topic, or issue?
- Vocabulary: Does the media use appropriate vocabulary, and can your students understand the language?
- Scenery and displays: Does the video show developmentally appropriate scenes?
- Quality: Is the piece of high quality, or does it experience any difficulties?

SHARE SLIDES AND POWERPOINT PRESENTATIONS

Many people use slides during their presentations. Slides can be effective tools when providing visual references. However, slide shows and PowerPoint presentations tend to get long and make the viewers sleepy. This can get worse when you add background music. Select slides carefully so that you are showing only the most essential ones to make your point or provide guidelines stipulating these expectations to your guest speakers. From an experienced teacher: "*My husband and I went to Japan on a three-week tour one summer. We created a presentation of twenty-five slides that we liked to show. He would come to the classroom for the presentation. We would begin by playing a tape of beautiful ancient Japanese music. We brought a large wall map and gave the viewers maps to mark the places we visited. Over the years, we shared our trip with students of all ages. The trick was moving quickly through the slides and using our two voices to keep the viewers alert.*"

INVITE GUEST SPEAKERS

Bringing guest speakers to the classroom is another way to help students make connections. Invite experts who specialize in particular areas or individuals who can offer particular insights about a specific social studies topic or issue. For example, you can invite a city government official to visit your classroom to talk about the government in general or a special responsibility within the city governance. A different example would be to invite a newspaper reporter who specializes in city government news. This is a perfect way to connect with your students, their families, and the community. It allows your students to hear from a variety of teachers, and you learn at the same time.

> *One time we had a guest speaker talk about China. It was a lot better than just reading about it because it was in terms we could understand and you [can] ask questions. He just talked about customs and cultures of China.*

> Robin, age 13, Grade 8

ARRANGE FOR GUEST SPEAKERS

Having guest speakers visit your class involves some risk. You cannot always preview the guest speaker as you would a video. Some of the guest speakers will have experience speaking to an audience and some will not. Some will be prepared, some will bring visual aids and/or handouts; others will not. Some guest speakers will know how to talk with your age group of students; other inexperienced speakers will need prompting ahead of them.

Guest Speaker Checklist

- Make an appointment to talk in person or on the telephone with the guest speaker. It is important that you hear the guest speaker talk so you can evaluate the quality of their voice, tone, and language skills.
- If the speaker has experience, ask if there is a videotape of a presentation for you to preview or if you can be in the audience at a forthcoming scheduled presentation.
- Be ready to ask some questions either directly or indirectly to learn more regarding their knowledge, skills, and dispositions about the:
    a. Content, processes, and vocabulary
    b. Outlook, biases, and agenda
    c. Communication skills applicable to your age group and students' special needs

- Discuss the length of time the guest speaker plans to talk, or tell the guest speaker how much time will be allotted. We suggest that you shorten the time by ten minutes to be sure the speaker stops and you have time to provide closure.
- Ask what visual aids and handouts, if appropriate, the speaker plans to bring and distribute.
- Find out if the speaker expects you to prepare the classroom setting in any way, order special equipment, make copies of the handout(s), and so forth.
- When you invite a guest speaker, be sure that each of you is clear on the date, time of arrival, length of the talk, classroom setting expectations, required equipment, and time the talk should end.
- Confirm the arrangements in writing by sending a letter or an e-mail message with copies sent to either your department chair or school administrator and a copy for you. (If you invite a guest speaker well in advance, be sure you make contact a few days prior to the speaking engagement to reconfirm the plans.)
- If the guest speaker has a business card or brochure, request that the guest speaker send you a copy in advance. Or ask the guest speaker to send you a résumé. You can use this information to introduce the guest speaker.
- After the presentation, send the guest speaker a letter of appreciation typed on school stationary. You can include hand written notes from your students if this is appropriate.

PREPARE STUDENTS TO
BE A RECEPTIVE AUDIENCE

Just as you would prepare your students when showing a video in your classroom, prepare your students when inviting guest speakers. Again, you are striving for a smooth sequence of learning experiences. We suggest that you tell your students about the guest speaker, what the guest speaker plans to address, and what you expect your students to do and learn.

You may want to dedicate a class session or part of a period to practice asking appropriate questions related to the topic or issue and determine the order of questions and who will ask them. Doing this will tell you what your students know, what they want to know, and how they plan to ask it. In this way you can add more background knowledge if you feel your students are not well informed and/or you are inviting a guest speaker who might address a controversial subject. For example, if you are asking a representative from the city council to talk about land use, you may or may not know in advance that your students (and their families) are opposed to moving the sports fields farther away. Perhaps you want to invite a guest speaker who will help your students to understand multiple perspectives related to an issue. Be sure you have alerted your guest speaker for a healthy conversation.

During the presentation, listen closely to what the guest speaker says. You may want to take notes to incorporate the key points into your overall unit of learning. Monitor the talk for accuracy, perceptions, and a point of view that you may need to explain later. As the speaker is talking, you may need to assist with the equipment, provide supplies, enhance with your own visuals, or redirect inappropriate student behaviors. We suggest you establish with your speaker that you will give them a five-minute warning sign to help them wrap-up on time. If your speaker does not heed the warning, then you must intervene at the one-minute warning and tell them in front of the group that there is one minute left. If that is not effective, you will have to say something kindly, such as, "That is where we will have to end today. Thank you Mr. or Ms. Guest Speaker."

In some cases, the guest speaker will leave before the class ends so you can close the learning with your students. In other cases, the guest speaker will join the audience and wait to leave when the students are dismissed. You will have to provide closure with the guest speaker in the classroom. You can ask students to write two or three main points on a card and share them in small groups to recap the talk. In both cases, you want to sound supportive of the guest speaker regardless of the talk. You can revisit the talk the next day to examine multiple points of view. You need to stay professional and polite at all times. Your guest speakers will be perceived experts in their fields, activists in the community, parents, or other individuals who your students know. You can decide if and when you want to invite your guest speakers back to speak with your classes.

If the guest you would like to invite isn't able to come to your room or to speak at an assembly, consider a Web chat or video conference. In one congressional district, the state senator held monthly chats with students via the Internet. The district coordinated the schedule for students.

TAKE FIELD TRIPS

Field trips offer one of the most effective ways to help your students learn about social studies. The field trip could be a walking trip or one that requires transportation, such as using vans, buses, or private cars. For example, you might be able to walk to a neighborhood business or agency who offers a small informational tour, such as the post office or courthouse. Many cities have local places of historic interest. You could partner with another teacher on your team so that two classes could go at one time and extend your time away from school for the two class sessions. Often it is school field trips that provide the unique opportunities for your students to leave their immediate neighborhoods. Otherwise your students might not ever see the local college, central park, beach, memorial or other site of community, and perhaps, state and national interest.

Unfortunately, taking field trips requires more time and money than most schools can allocate. However, certain agencies and organizations will reimburse bus transportation. You may be allowed to take only one or two field trips per school year, so choose wisely. The trips may be selected as a team, grade level, or social studies department on a rotating schedule, with a different subject area or a different aspect of social studies featured each year. Field trips usually are identified early in the school year so detailed arrangements can be made well in advance, coordinated with curriculum and instruction.

FOLLOW GUIDELINES FOR TAKING FIELD TRIPS

There are several factors to keep in mind when planning field trips:

1. Identify some locations fairly close to the school. The less time you spend getting there, the more time you can spend being there.

2. Know the purpose for selecting particular sites. Everyone wants to know that you are spending time and money efficiently and effectively.

3. Select sites that most students have not or would not visit on their own or with their families.

4. Contact the potential sites to make appointments to visit them. You will want to investigate:

   a. Alignment of standards and expectations with the field trip experience
   b. Availability of a tour guide
   c. Content and vocabulary quality of the displays and tour guides
   d. If the tour includes experiential, hands-on learning and any materials such as brochures or worksheets
   e. Choices, costs, and lengths of tours
   f. Easy access for buses to drop off passengers and park
   g. Easy access to restrooms
   h. Convenient place(s) to eat sack lunches and dispose of trash
   i. Predominance of souvenir shops and how you can avoid them
   j. Procedures for arranging a field trip

5. Know both the procedures and paperwork at your school for arranging a field trip, including transportation, chaperones, admission fees, and permission slips.

Inform students of both the content related to taking this particular field trip and the behaviors to be used during the field trip. You need to make the consequences for not complying with expectations quite clear to students and their parents.

Leading study tours with students is a fabulous way to extend the walls of the classroom for authentic experiences. Many teachers choose to take educational tours with students to supplement and enrich their courses of study. These types of trips provide unique opportunities for students' personal growth in ways you can never create in your classroom.

CONSIDER VIRTUAL FIELD TRIPS

When time and funds are scarce, consider virtual field trips through broadcast television or the Internet. Colonial Williamsburg, for example, offers programming through PBS and satellite, videos,

DVDs, as well as the Internet (See www.history.org/history/teaching/eft.cfm). Many museums host their own sites. Alternately, you can have your students plan virtual field trips as a project involving technology.

One set of sites that we want to emphasize is the Presidential Libraries and Museums. You can find the home page at www.archives.gov/presidential-libraries/. Most students enjoy learning more about the U.S. presidents; an abundance of information along with virtual tours can be found at this Web site.

HIGHLIGHT CAREERS

Everything you teach is based on one or more academic disciplines with people who have dedicated their lives and developed professional careers to preserve, communicate, and advance that particular field of study. Each field of study is filled with all kinds of careers either directly or indirectly related to it. Grab these teachable moments to make the connections between the social studies established concepts and practices and future educational and career possibilities. Frequently it is a teacher who showed an object, invited a guest speaker, or took the students on a field trip that serves as the catalyst to the future. Your use of resources may provide just the rationale your students need to invest in their learning or to explore social studies–related careers later in their lives.

Career education is easily integrated in class activities during each unit. Consider making a chart per unit or one continuous chart that you and your students maintain throughout the semester or school year. Students can contribute ideas throughout the unit of learning as they make connections to the community and the world. You might want to invite guest speakers who are professionals within the subject area, such as the genealogy librarian or individuals who know about these kinds of careers, such as a professor of history or library science from the local community college or university.

From a veteran teacher: *"I like inviting the students' parents into the classroom to talk about their careers. This is the first time many of the students have heard their parents talk or really learned what their parents know and do. I spread the visits out throughout the year."*

CHECK OUT COMMUNITY RESOURCES

As you travel around your district and follow the local news, you will become aware of significant features or places of notable interest and potential personalities in your local area. See Table 9.1 for a list of potential community resources.

Table 9.1 Community Resources

airport	city/county planning office	highway patrol	police station
apiary	courthouse	historical site	recycling center
aquarium	cultural center	hospital	retail store
archeological site	dairy	industrial plant	sanitation center
art gallery	dam	legislature session	sawmill/lumber yard
assembly plant	dock/ harbor	library	shoreline
bank	factory	mass transit authority	telecommunications company
book publisher	farm	military installation	town meeting
bookstore	fire department	mine	train station
broadcasting station	fish hatchery	monuments	university
buildings	foreign embassy	museum	utility company
bus station	forest	newspaper plant	water reservoir
canal lock	gas company	observatory	wildlife reserve
capitol	geological site	oil refinery	weather bureau
cemetery	health department	park	zoo

START A SCHOOL RESOURCE BANK

Some of your best resources will be your colleagues and your students' families. As you learn more about the people with whom you are working as well as the resources in the community, start a resource bank (Epstein, 1997). You can achieve this electronically or by hand using note cards and a small file box. You will want to record valuable information to reference in the future when you plan your curriculum and get ready to start your instruction.

Design a note card that fits your purposes. Perhaps colleagues have already begun this for you and you can use their banks to begin. See Table 9.2 for a list of information to gather from parents and members of the community to start a social studies school resource bank.

Table 9.2   Resource Bank File Card Template

1. Area(s) of knowledge, expertise, or travel:
2. Type of presentation:
3. Length of presentation:
4. Required equipment:
5. Time needed for notification to prepare presentation:
6. Name:
7. E-mail Address:
8. Telephone Numbers:
9. Your child's name, if applicable:
10. Your child's social studies teacher's name, if applicable:

Become a Role Model of Resourcefulness . . .

Whether you are aware of your influence or not, how you interact with social studies resources will communicate volumes to your students that you could not teach any other way. From one teacher: *"I teach geography and love maps of all kinds. I have 200 different kinds of maps in my collection. The students can touch and use some of my maps; however, some of my maps are just to be viewed. I even have a few special maps that I keep at home and share only photographs of the maps with my students. I can see the looks on my students' faces as I talk about my maps and continue bringing more maps throughout the school year. One student told me that he always thought maps were nerdy until he watched how I cherished the maps and what I could learn from them."*

These same kinds of reactions will occur as you model to your students how to handle realia (especially precious objects), how to ask questions either as general or philosophical inquiries of specific guests, and how to make connections between prior learning and new explorations. Incorporating a variety of resources into your social studies classes will help your students see the presence and power of social studies everywhere and learn to become resourceful themselves. We strongly encourage you to consider your responsibilities as a role model seriously. These opportunities will establish a keen sense and orientation about the world for your students now and as lifelong learners.

Resources for social studies abound. The secret is when you shop, travel, or visit the library or a museum, keep your units of learning in mind. With time and experience, you will refine your abilities and expertise to ask your students to suggest and bring in resources too. These next steps will reflect your growth in letting the themes, topics, and issues spark the imaginations of your students as they develop their understanding, application, and appreciation of the social studies. While this chapter examined physical resources and guest speakers, Chapter 10 presents using technological resources in the classroom with suggestions on how to use technology as well as a reference list of Web sites by subject area.

Suggested Activities

1. Visit a teacher supply store or thumb through social studies supply catalogs to find resources you might want to order or to initiate ideas for future resources.

2. Talk with other social studies teachers to find out how they use and store their resources.

3. Obtain a list of your school's videos and CDs/DVDs and begin to preview ones you think would be appropriate for a unit of learning.

4. Attend a state or national social studies conference and acquire all kinds of resources and resource ideas.

CHAPTER TEN

Integrate Technology to Enrich Learning

Given the complexity of social studies with the range of academic disciplines and diversity of teaching strategies, we have dedicated an entire chapter to Internet resources and integrating technology. We offer many practical guidelines that may be helpful for you now as you begin to expand your repertoire and teach new classes or grade levels (Risinger, 1996). With the increase in school desktop and laptop computers as well as handheld devices, teachers and students have additional tools for information and communication in the classroom. The digitizing of new as well as historical information is constantly taking place. Consider the wealth of resources from the Library of Congress and National Archives collections, which are now available online.

TAKE A TECHNOLOGY INVENTORY

Determine what types of technology are available to you. Do you have any equipment in your room? Do you have an overhead projector? An ELMO electronic imager? A multimedia computer? Most schools today have at least one computer in the classroom, although it may not be a new one. You may or may not have a projection system. If you have a television monitor, you can project from your computer with a cable device, such as a TVator. This will enable your whole class or a large group to view the screen at one time, rather than having small groups crowd around the computer monitor. Perhaps you have a few computers in your room that students can use by themselves or in pairs. Hopefully you have ready access.

Sometimes equipment is shared among teachers. Your school may have a traveling cart of laptops or AlphaSmarts, for example. Or you may need to reserve time in a media center or a computer lab. In these situations you will have to plan ahead to coordinate scheduling with your lessons.

Another factor in your planning will be to determine the level of proficiency of your students and what the expectations are for you in terms of their technology proficiency development. Does your school require students to take computer classes that address the International Society for Technology in Education (ISTE) standards (2000), or will it be your responsibility to incorporate such lessons into your teaching? These standards include demonstrating basic operations, understanding ethical and other issues, and using tools to record information, produce work, communicate with others, conduct research, solve problems, and make decisions.

Your school district and/or your school may have policies and procedures for you to follow as well. Most districts have filtering software that prevents your students from accessing inappropriate sites. Most likely, they also have established an Acceptable Use Policy (AUP) for all students and employees about what is appropriate and inappropriate behavior with respect to using computers and the Web, including e-mail communication.

DETERMINE YOUR COMPUTER USE

How you use technology and the Internet will depend on expectations, time, space, abilities of the students, and your expertise. Consider the following ways to integrate technology (Kottler & Gallavan, 2007).

Demonstration for Whole Group Instruction—The screen or monitor is placed where all the students can see the display. The teacher guides the students through the content. Students participate firsthand in the experiential learning by posing inquiries, guiding the operations, recording data, and analyzing outcomes.

Cooperative Group Station—The computer is located to one side or in a corner of the classroom where a small group of students can gather around it. Groups may be working on the same or different parts of the same unit of learning and will share results with one another. Time is given during the day for different groups to work at the station; the teacher can assist each group.

Learning Centers—Different forms of instructional technology are located to the sides or in the corners of the classroom where individuals or small groups can work. Assignments at the learning centers can be related to the units of learning directly or indirectly. All students can go to any learning center at once at your direction, or the students may go to their assigned centers when they have completed other tasks.

Independent Research/Communication Stations—Computers are located to the sides or in the corners of the classroom where one to three students can work as they desire. Sign-up sheets will ensure equitable access and use. Factors to consider include length of time at stations, supplies needed, and measurements of productivity.

Computer Lab—Computers are located in such a way that each student has individual access to a computer at the same time. The social studies teacher or the computer teacher leads students through lessons giving time for personalized practice and application. Students may work on individual or group projects.

TEACH WITH TECHNOLOGY

Teaching with technology is a three-prong expectation. First, you want to know how to use the computer to find information for yourself and with your students. You want to be able to find information on the Internet by conducting a search. You can search general Web sites or you may have access to a professional library, such as an electronic library for students. This is one way for you to keep up with the latest research.

You also want to find information using your own computer files. Information may be accessed from a word processing program, spreadsheet, PowerPoint presentation, or attached e-mail documents. You may be given information on a disk, CD, or a memory stick that you need and want to use to prepare lessons to teach to your students or for your students to use to find information for themselves.

A second way to teach with technology is how you record and store information related to curricular preparation and classroom management that you both add to and originate. You can use word processing programs to create your own documents, spreadsheets, slide presentations, and so forth.

Some of you will use technology for administrative purposes. In many schools, teachers record students' grades and attendance electronically. Announcements are now posted digitally. You may even find forms that you need to complete and return electronically too.

The third way to teach with technology is how you present and share information. Many of you will have access to large viewing screens where you can project Internet sites to read together as a whole class. You might have SMART Boards where you can interact with the Internet site by touching the screen. You can share information using PowerPoint and other slide presentation systems, ELMO and other projection systems, and overhead transparencies.

Many schools are acquiring interactive software where students can respond to prompts or questions with hand-held response mechanisms frequently known as clickers and have results automatically presented in charts and displays in PowerPoint presentations. For example, students can vote, take a position, rank items, or answer questions on an issue. This technology helps keep students involved in direct instruction. It can also be used to check entry-level knowledge about a topic and to make quick assessments.

Each of the three ways of teaching with technology is not just for you to use to deliver information to your students. Each of the three ways also should be taught to your students for their uses. We recommend that you talk with your technology teacher to examine ways of integrating your curriculum and instruction. You may discover that you can collaborate on your projects to equip your students with authentic and exciting outcomes.

Students enjoy "surfing the Web" and certainly this type of exploration will be beneficial, but it can be very time consuming without meaningful results aligned with your learning outcomes. Therefore, most teachers preselect what they consider to be "good Web sites" from which students can choose to conduct research. Narrowing the search will economize on time and offer viable choices for students.

From a veteran teacher: *"I like to show my students how to make charts, graphs, tables, and other graphic organizers. They think it is a great way to share information and not write another report."*

EVALUATE WEB SITES CRITICALLY

You and your students want to be able to scan a Web site quickly and critically to see if the information you are seeking is available, if the Web site offers creative possibilities to expand one's thinking, and if the Web site is safe and trustworthy. Here are five groups of questions to ask when looking at Web sites:

Evaluating a Web Site

1. What can you learn from the URL description before navigating to the Web site? What is the domain? Who is the publisher? Is it a personal page?

2. What is listed on the Home Page? How current is the information? Who is the organization or author? What are the organization's or author's credentials?

3. What is the quality of the information on the Web site? Can you see and understand the pictures and words easily? What kinds of links are available? Can you navigate in and out of the Web site readily? Is the information research based and authentic? Does the information have footnotes and citations?

4. What do others say about the Web site? Are there links to other resources? Are there links to reputable reviews?

5. What is your reaction to the Web site? What is the purpose of the Web site? Does the Web site fulfill or exceed your expectations?

Remember that information on Web sites is self-published.

We suggest you visit http://school.discovery.com/schrock guide/eval.html to guide you in evaluating Web sites that you may want to access for yourself and with your students. Kathy Schrock's "Guide for Educators" has evaluation surveys at the elementary, middle, and secondary school levels. There are also evaluation forms for blogs and podcasts that are easy to use and student-friendly.

LOOK AT GENERAL SOCIAL STUDIES RESOURCES

There are many wonderful Internet sites to consider. Look for virtual field trips, WebQuests, and simulations, as well as digitized primary and secondary resources to enrich your students' learning. You'll find music, sheet music, movies, speeches, newspapers, magazines, maps, time lines, pictures of art and architecture, photography, diaries, journals, documentaries, maps, and encyclopedia information. It's no secret; it's all at your fingertips. Listed below we have categorized some of the Internet sites with which we have had positive experiences.

General Resources

Indiana Social Studies Resources: *http://education.indiana .edu/~socialst*

Multicultural Holidays: *www.educationworld.com/a_sites/ sites067.shtml*

Religions of the World: *www.bbc.co.uk/religion/religions*

Social Studies: *http://wdcrobcolp01.ed.gov/cfapps/free/display subject.cfm?sid=9*

Social Studies Resources/Lesson Plans: *www.csun.edu/ ~hcedu013*

Teaching Tolerance: *www.tolerance.org*

Media

A&E Biographies: *www.biography.com*

ABC News: *www.abcnews.go.com*

AFI Movies: *www.100movies.com*

Annenberg Media/CPI: *www.learner.org/exhibits*

Awesome Library: *www.awesomelibrary.org*

CNN News: *www.cnn.com*

Encyclopedia Britannica: *www.britannica.com*

Future State: *www.future.state.gov*

History Channel: *www.historychannel.com*

Infoplease: *www.infoplease.com*

Internet Public Library: *www.ipl.org/div/news*

MSNBC News: *www.msnbc.com/news*

Newsweek: *www.newsweekeducation.com/index.php*

PBS: *www.pbs.org*

Scholastic: *www.scholastic.com/sitemap.htm*

Time: *www.time.com/time/2006/time100*

Museums (Many museums have educational trunks available.)

American Museum of Natural History: *www.amnh.org*

Carnegie Museum of Natural History: *www.carnegiemuseums.org/cmnh*

Field Museum, Chicago: *www.fieldmuseum.org*

Holocaust Museum, Houston: *www.hmh.org/ed_high_school_1.asp*

Maxwell Museum of Anthropology, Albuquerque, N.M.: *www.unm.edu/~maxwell/traveling_trunk_exhibits.html*

Marietta Museum of History trunk, Marietta, Ga.: *www.mariettahistory.org/trunkshows.htm*

Museum Hotlist: *http://sln.fi.edu/tfi/hotlists/museums.html*

National Civil Rights Museum: *www.civilrightsmuseum.org*

National Holocaust Museum: *www.ushmm.org*

Smithsonian Institute: *www.si.edu*

U.S. Agencies and Departments

Census Bureau: *www.census.gov*

Census Gazetteer: *www.census.gov/cgi-bin/gazetteer*

Central Intelligence Agency: *www.odci.gov*

Federal Bureau of Intelligence: *www.fbi.gov*

Fed Stats: *www.fedstats.gov*

Institute of Peace: *www.usip.org*

Library of Congress: *www.loc.gov/index.html*

Mint: *www.usmint.gov/index.cfm?flash=yes*

National Security Agency: *www.nsa.gov*

Pentagon: *www.pentagon.gov*

Peace Corps: *www.peacecorps.gov/wws*

Project Visa: *www.projectvisa.com*

Selective Service: *www.sss.gov*

UNICEF: *www.unicef.org/voy*

U.S. Department of Agriculture: *www.usda.gov/wps/portal/usdahome*

U.S. Department of Commerce: *www.commerce.gov*

U.S. Department of Defense: *www.defenselink.mil*

U.S. Department of Education: *www.ed.gov/index.jhtml*

U.S. Department of Energy: *www.energy.gov*

U.S. Department of Health and Human Services: *www.hhs.gov*

U.S. Department of Homeland Security: *www.dhs.gov/dhspublic*

U.S. Department of Housing and Urban Development: *www.hud.gov*

U.S. Department of Justice: *www.usdoj.gov*

U.S. Department of Labor: *www.dol.gov*

U.S. Department of State: *www.state.gov*

U.S. Department of Transportation: *www.dot.gov*

U.S. Department of Treasury: *www.treasury.gov*

U.S. Department of Veterans Affairs: *www.va.gov*

U.S. House of Representatives: *www.house.gov*

U.S. Senate: *www.senate.gov*

U.S. Supreme Court: *www.supremecourtus.gov*

The White House: *www.whitehouse.gov*

JUDGE CIVICS RESOURCES

American Bar Association: *www.abanet.org/publiced/webresources.html*

The American Promise: *www.farmers.com/FarmComm/AmericanPromise*

Ben's Guide to US Government: *http://bensguide.gpo.gov*

Center for Civic Education: *www.civiced.org*

Conflict Management: *www.triune.ca*

Congress for Kids: *www.congressforkids.net*

Congressional E-mail Directory: *www.webslingerz.com/jhoffman/congress-email.html*

Constitution Day: *www.justicelearning.org/constitutionday/index.asp*

Constitution Day Resources: *http://usgovinfo.about.com/blconstday.htm*

Constitution Facts: *www.constitutionfacts.com*

Constitution of the United States: *www.law.emory.edu/cms/site/index.php?id=3080*

Constitutional Center: *www.constitutionday.us/educators.htm*

Constitutional Rights Foundation: *www.crf-usa.org*

Elections: *www.edgate.com/elections/inactive*

Federal Government Resources: *www.lib.umich.edu/govdocs/fedhis.html*

First Gov for Kids: *www.kids.gov*

Gov Spot: *www.govspot.com*

Kids Voting USA ®: *www.kidsvotingusa.org/*

Landmark Supreme Court Cases: *www.landmarkcases.org*

Law Day; The American Bar Association: *www.abanet.org/* (Search "Law Day")

League of Women Voters: *www.lwv.org//AM/Template.cfm? Section=Home*

Library of Congress Thomas Legislative Center: *http://thomas.loc.gov/*

Mock Trial Matters: *www.nationalmocktrial.org/index.cfm*

National Constitution Center: *www.constitutioncenter.org/education/WelcomeEducatorsandStudents/index.shtml*

National Student/Parent Mock Election: *www.nationalmockelection.org*

Political Resources on the Net: *www.politicalresources.net*

Rock the Vote: *www.rockthevote.org*

State Government Information: *www.loc.gov/rr/news/stategov/stategov.html*

This Day in History: *www.historychannel.com/today*

United Nations: *www.un.org*

United Nations Cyber School Bus: *www.un.org/Pubs/ CyberSchoolBus*

Youth for Justice; Office of Juvenile Justice and Delinquency Prevention and five national organizations (American Bar Association, Center for Civic Education, Constitutional Rights Foundation, Phi Alpha Delta, and Street Law, Inc.: *www .youthforjustice.org*

WEIGH ECONOMIC RESOURCES

Center for Entrepreneur and Economic Education:*www .umsl.edu/~econed*

EcEdWeb: *http://ecedweb.unomaha.edu/home.htm*

Economics Challenge—The Federal Reserve Stock Market Game: *www.smgww.org*

Federal Reserve Bank of San Francisco: *www.frbsf.org/ education/index.html*

Junior Achievement: *www.ja.org/nested/santaclara*

Job Shadow Day: *www.jobshadow.org*

North American Association for Environmental Education: *http://eelink.net/pages/EE-Link+Introduction*

Technology at Home: *www.pbs.org/wgbh/aso/tryit/tech*

Wise Pockets: *www.umsl.edu/~wpockets*

MAP OUT GEOGRAPHY RESOURCES

Activities and Reading and the Geography of the United States (ARGUS): *www.aag.org/ARGUS/ARGUS.html*

Atlapedia Online: *www.atlapedia.com*

Country Reports: *www.countryreports.org*

Culture Quest World Tour: *www.ipl.org/div/kidspace/cquest*

Environmental Ed: *http://edugreen.teri.res.in*

Flags: *www.flags.net/indexu.htm*

Flags of All Countries: *www.wave.net/upg/immigration/flags.html*

Geo-Images Project: *http://geoimages.berkeley.edu*

National Geographic: *www.nationalgeographic.com/index.html*

National Geographic Bee: *www.nationalgeographic.com/geographybee*

National Parks Services: *www.nps.gov*

States and Capitals: *www.50states.com*

U.S. Community Atlas (ESRI): *www.esri.com/industries/k–12/atlas/index.html*

USGS: *www.usgs.gov*

World Fact book (CIA): *www.cia.gov/cia/publications/factbook/index.html*

EXAMINE HISTORY RESOURCES

Abraham Lincoln: *http://members.aol.com/RVSNorton/Lincoln.html*

Abraham Lincoln Online: *http://showcase.netins.net/web/creative/lincoln.html*

African American History: *http://historicaltextarchive.com/sections.php?op=listarticles&secid=8*

African American Mosaic: *www.loc.gov/exhibits/african/intro.html*

American Civil War: *www.theteachersguide.com/Civilwarlessons.html; http://americancivilwar.com/civil.html*

American Treasures: *www.loc.gov/exhibits/treasures/trr001.html*

Black History: *www.kn.pacbell.com/wired/BHM/AfroAm.html*

Black History Tour: *http://library.thinkquest.org/10320/Tourmenu.htm*

Early American History: *http://earlyamerica.com*

Ellis Island: *www.ellisisland.org*

Eyewitness History: *www.ibiscom.com*

First Ladies of the White House: *www.whitehouse.gov/history/firstladies/index.html*

Hispanic Heritage: *http://teacher.scholastic.com/activities/hispanic/index.htm*

HistoryNet: *www.historynet.com*

The History Place: *www.historyplace.com*

Historical Text Archive: *www.historicaltextarchive.com*

Immigration: *www.pbs.org/independentlens/newamericans*

A More Perfect Union: Japanese Americans and the U.S. Constitution: *http://americanhistory.si.edu/perfectunion/experience/index.html*

Library of Congress Presents America's Stories: *www.americaslibrary.gov*

Library of Congress Veteran History Project: *www.loc.gov/vets*

The National Archives: *www.archives.gov/index.html*

National Endowment for the Humanities EdSitement: *http://edsitement.neh.gov*

National History Day; The National Endowment for the Humanities: *www.nationalhistoryday.org*

National Women's History Project: *www.nwhp.org*

Native American Sites: *www.nativeculturelinks.com/indians.html*

Native Web: *www.nativeweb.org*

Oral History: *http://alpha.dickinson.edu/oha*

Oregon Trail: *www.isu.edu/~trinmich/Oregontrail.html*

U.S. Historical Documents: *www.law.ou.edu/hist/*

U.S. Historical Documents Archives: *www.ushda.org*

U.S. Presidents: *www.ipl.org/div/POTUS*

Western U.S. History: *www.pbs.org/weta/thewest*

World History Links: *http://historylink101.com*

SEEK PEDAGOGICAL RESOURCES

Ben's Guide for Kids: *http://bensguide.gpo.gov*

Dave's ESOL Cafe: *www.eslcafe.com*

Discovery School: *http://school.discovery.com/schrockguide/history/histg.html*

Diversity Calendar: *www3.kumc.edu/diversity*

EdGate : *www.edgate.com/discovery.html*

Federal Resources for Educational Excellence: *www.ed.gov/free /index.html*

History/Social Studies Web Sites for K–12 Teachers: *http://k–12historysocialstudies.com/boals.html*

National Center for Educational Statistics: *http://nces.ed.gov/help/sitemap.asp*

National Center for History in the Schools: *www.sscnet.ucla.edu/nchs*

National Council for History Education: *www.garlandind.com/nche*

National Geographic Lessons (Grades 5–8): *www.nationalgeographic.com/resources/ngo/education/ideas58/index.html*

National Geographic Lessons (Grades 9–12): *www.nationalgeographic.com/resources/ngo/education/ideas912/index.html*

School House Rock: *www.school-house-rock.com/Prea.html*

SCORE History/Social Science: *http://score.rims.k12.ca.us*

Social Studies School Service: *www.socialstudies.com*

Social Studies Lesson Plans and Resources: *www.cloudnet.com/ ~edrbsass/edsoc.htm*

Teaching With Documents: *www.edteck.com/dbq*

Teaching With Political Cartoons: *http://cagle.msnbc.com/teacher*

Texas Education Network: *www.tenet.edu*

FOLLOW NCSS TECHNOLOGY GUIDELINES

Technology guidelines for the social studies have been divided into five distinct areas (Mason et al., 2000, pp. 107–116) that include:

1. "Extending learning beyond what could be accomplished without technology" in ways that are practical and relevant

2. "Introducing technology in context" as a tool for learning social studies content and skills

3. "Include opportunities for students to study relationships among science, technology, and society," examining the benefits and risks of new technologies

4. "Foster the development of the skills, knowledge, and participation as good citizens in a democratic society" to revitalize citizenship education, provide multiple current perspectives on controversial issues, and promote social and political involvement for civic action locally and globally

5. "Contribute to the research and evaluation of social studies and technology" advancing the purposes of social studies

Members of NCSS developed a position statement and guidelines for social studies educators based on the National Educational Technology Standards to promote the integration of technology into practice and identify resources (NCSS Position Statement, 2006). The main ideas fall into five categories:

Technology Operations and Concepts

1. Demonstrate a sound understanding of technology operations and concepts as they relate to social studies education

2. Demonstrate introductory knowledge, skills, and understanding of concepts related to technology

3. Demonstrate continual growth in technology knowledge and skills to stay abreast of current and emerging technologies

Planning and Designing Learning Environments and Experiences

1. Plan and design effective social studies learning environments and experiences supported by technology

2. Design developmentally appropriate learning opportunities that apply technology-enhanced instructional strategies to support the diverse needs of learners

3. Apply current research on teaching and learning with technology when planning learning environments and experiences

4. Identify and locate technology resources and evaluate them for accuracy and suitability

5. Plan for the management of technology resources within the context of learning activities relevant to your social studies topics and issues

6. Plan strategies to manage student learning in a technology-enhanced environment

Teaching, Learning, and the Curriculum

1. Implement curriculum plans that include methods and strategies for applying technology to maximize student learning in social studies

2. Facilitate technology-enhanced experiences that address content standards and student technology standards

3. Use technology to support learner-centered strategies that address the diverse needs of students

4. Apply technology to develop students' higher-order skills and creativity

5. Manage student learning activities in a technology-enhanced environment

Assessment and Evaluation

1. Apply technology through a variety of strategies to assess and evaluate student learning in social studies

2. Apply technology in assessing student learning of subject matter using a variety of assessment techniques

3. Use technology resources to collect and analyze data, interpret results, and communicate findings to improve instructional practices and maximize student learning

4. Apply multiple methods of evaluation to determine students' appropriate uses of technology resources

Social, Ethical, Legal, and Human Issues

1. Model and teach legal and ethical practices related to technology uses

2. Apply technology resources to enable and empower learners with diverse backgrounds, characteristics, and abilities

3. Identify and use technology resources that affirm diversity

4. Promote safe and healthy uses of technology resources

5. Facilitate equitable access to technology resources for all students

VARY TECHNOLOGY EXPERIENCES

There are many ways to integrate technology. Below we share sample activities based on information from the U.S. Citizenship and Immigration Service (USCIS) Web site at www.uscis.gov/portal/site/uscis that will be relevant for most classes. Here you will find sample questions for individuals who want to become U.S.

citizens to try before they take their actual test along with vast amounts of other information. Discuss the answers with your students. This is an excellent Web site to introduce to your social studies students.

In Box 10.1 you will find five different technology learning experiences. Use your imagination to think of additional developmentally appropriate applications and extensions.

Box 10.1   Five Technology Learning Examples

Use the United States Citizenship and Immigration Services' Web site at www.uscis.gov/ as a reference.

1. Ask your students to complete a specified number of questions. You can organize this assignment as a whole group with each student typing on a computer or with students collaborating with a partner in a computer lab situation. Or if you have access to only a few or one computer in your classroom, you can make this assignment with students working in small groups, as a center activity, or individually throughout the week.

2. Give your students the citizenship test either on the computer or on paper. After reviewing the responses, assign a question to each student or groups of students to research and present to the class as a discussion.

3. Provide your students with population, immigration, or citizenship data to enter on a database spreadsheet and transfer into charts, tables, and figures to see trends. Use graphing calculators, if available.

4. Show your students how to create a PowerPoint presentation to share their information from item #3 or their data from item #3, or both, with the rest of the class.

5. E-mail a peer, relative, researcher, civic worker, journalist, new immigrant, or other individual with specific questions to enhance your students' research on citizenship, immigration, and population in your immediate geographic region, state, or the nation.

Keep Social Studies at Your Fingertips . . .

We find that most students are fascinated with the abundance of resources available on the Internet. The field of social studies includes every aspect of our lives, and the Internet allows us access to rich and diverse resources to inform and support our teaching in every way. We think you will discover all these secrets and "bookmark" your own favorites soon. In the next chapter we will identify by subject area the professional organizations that support social studies education and their Web sites as we suggest other ways to develop your professional expertise.

Suggested Activities

1. Develop specific rubrics for your students to reference to evaluate particular Web sites.

2. Talk with your technology teacher to develop strategies to apply technology to maximize student learning in one of your units.

3. Identify and bookmark a few Web sites that you will frequently use for your social studies courses. Be sure to consider teaching sites too.

4. See what activities you can find on the Internet to enhance your curriculum, instruction, and assessments.

C H A P T E R   E L E V E N

Seek Powerful Activities *to Engage Learners*

T eaching social studies is both exhilarating and exhausting! You are tackling the most challenging content knowledge that includes more depth, breadth, and diversity than any other subject area with an audience of secondary students. Plus it changes every day. We encourage you to look for ways that make your classes meaningful, integrated, value based, challenging, and active as mentioned in Chapter 3. A central component to all of these endeavors is making social studies real by extending it beyond your classroom and the textbook. In addition to all of the strategies, resources, and Web sites shared with you in previous chapters, this chapter contains suggestions for activities that you can incorporate either into your teaching, at your school, or within your school district and state. Choose ones that you feel will benefit your students.

PARTICIPATE IN PROGRAMS AND COMPETITIONS

From a department chair: *"My involvement in Project Citizen began when I was asked to serve on a judging panel. I was amazed at the research the students had done on the topic of school recycling and their proposal to reduce waste in the school, especially paper! These students had the background and poise to answer several questions the panel members posed. This was inspiration for me to learn more about the program."*

There are myriad programs, contests, and competitions within and across academic disciplines. Most are free, some cost a little, and a few are expensive. Explore the ones that seem interesting to you. Talk to teachers whose students participate in these activities about their experiences. Watch how their students demonstrate their expertise through new knowledge, refined skills, and positive dispositions as a result of their involvement.

Many of the programs mentioned below have developed and published activities that correlate with state content standards and the national themes. Many programs have teacher-prepared lesson plans and even curricular guidelines for you to follow or adapt for your students. These will help you in the selection of materials and lessons for your students. The supplemental curriculum may already be approved by your state or district. You'll find local and state contacts eager to have you participate.

To get started, conduct some research on the Web; attend a local professional development workshop or a presentation at a local, state, regional, or national conference; it is best to see the contest or competition in person. You can go it alone or partner with another teacher. While space prevents great detail, a short summary of a variety of opportunities for students with educational support for teachers is provided below. This is not meant to be a comprehensive list. These are programs that you will hear mentioned at local and state social studies conferences and read about in the newspaper. The class time needed for these activities may range from a few sessions to on-going time throughout the school year. Or, you may want to start a social studies club and meet with students on a regular basis after the school day ends.

SHOWCASE CIVICS AND GOVERNMENT ACTIVITIES

We the People: The Citizen and the Constitution—Offered through the Center for Civic Education, is a set of curricular materials that has produced an increase in student achievement and a sense of civic responsibility when implemented in the classroom. The program is organized for students in Grades 4–12 with texts available at three levels: upper elementary, middle school, and high school. The curriculum focuses on the history and principles of our constitutional democracy experienced through a series of critical thinking activities that utilize cooperative learning. Through these exercises, students practice the skills of responsible citizenship. The culminating activity is a simulated congressional hearing. For dedicated students, there is a national competition at the high school level with the final hearings held in Washington, D.C., in the spring.

Teachers' guides are available as are assessment materials. Intensive summer institutes for teachers are held annually. Workshops are held throughout the country and in other locations as well. Programs, publications, research, and resources, plus professional development information can be found at www.civiced.org.

We the People: Project Citizen—This program for middle school students encourages participation at the local and state government levels. As a class or in small groups, students study a public policy issue and present their findings in portfolios. The culminating activity is to present the portfolio(s) to another class, parents, and/or members of the community, as well as other authentic audiences. Student portfolios may be submitted to a local showcase and, if selected, proceed to the state showcase and then to the national summer showcase. Project Citizen is a collaborative effort of the Center for Civic Education and the National Conference of State Legislatures. Student materials also are available in Spanish. Again, there are workshops for teachers throughout the country. See www.civiced.org/project_citizen.php.

Mock Trial—To improve communication and literacy skills and to increase appreciation for the law and the American judicial system, teachers often bring mock trials to their classrooms. From *Goldilocks and the Three Bears* to specially written cases, students enjoy simulating trials as they develop public speaking skills.

Beginning in 1984 in Des Moines, Iowa, National Mock Trial Competition has expanded and continues to include more states and countries as it moves from state to state each spring. The competition is governed by the Rules of the Competition and the National High School Mock Trial Rules of Evidence. Students work with their teacher coaches and local attorneys to prepare cases for which they serve as attorneys, plaintiffs, and defendants. Cases are held in real courtrooms with real judges. There is a library of mock trials for teachers to use in preparation with their classes. *Mock Trial Matters,* the annual newsletter, and other information are available at www.nationalmocktrial.org/index.cfm.

Constitution Day—As of 2005, all institutions receiving federal funding must celebrate Constitution Day on September 17. The Constitutional Rights Foundation has a variety of print and online materials for students in Grades 4–12. Other helpful resources are available from the Library of Congress, the National Archives, the National Constitution Center, and the Bill of Rights Institute. The Constitutional Rights Foundation publishes a free quarterly newsletter with lessons on U.S. history, world history, and government.

Law Day—In 1957, the president of the American Bar Association (ABA) began to lay the foundation for a day to honor the legal system. President Eisenhower proclaimed the first Law Day as May 1, 1958, and in 1961, Congress passed a resolution. The ABA celebrates Law Day each year with a different theme. The ABA provides a planning guide and ample suggestions for programs including essay, photo, and poster contests. Lessons and promotional materials are readily available. Go to http://www .abanet.org/ and search "Law Day." Your state bar association will also be a good resource for you.

Teens, Crime, and the Community—The National Crime Prevention Council helps teens explore issues of crime and develop strategies to prevent crime in their neighborhoods with the Teens, Crime, and the Community initiative. *Community Works* looks at violence and youth-related issues in a series of lessons ranging from substance abuse to conflict management. It focuses on making schools safer and reducing the potential for victimization. *Youth Safety Corps* provides a structure for ongoing participation in activities in which students partner with school and community personnel on selected projects, such as making presentations for elementary students or cleaning up schools. Student leadership and team building skills are emphasized by the Youth Safety Corps.

Two regional workshops are held each year for teachers. Half-day and full-day workshops are offered on various topics such as bullying and intimidation, substance abuse, and adult and youth partnerships. You can find more specific information at www.ncpc .org/programs/tcc/About.php.

Street Law—Ever since 1972, Street Law, Inc. has worked to help young people become successful, civic-minded citizens in schools, juvenile justice, and other settings by creating programs on law, democracy, and human rights. For high school teachers, a practical law textbook has been developed. Lesson plans, case studies, mock trials, and other resources are available online. Some university law school students receive credit for co-teaching *Street Law*. Check in your area to see if a law school near you offers this program. Some high schools offer *Street Law* as an elective course. For information, go to www.streetlaw.org/content .asp? ContentId=158.

Parents and the Law—In 1996, Street Law, Inc. offered the first Teen Parent and the Law program. Teachers with pregnant and parenting students will find that the Parents and the Law curriculum addresses the challenges their students frequently face. Annual workshops are available to support teachers in the delivery of this 23-lesson curriculum designed to help students understand how the law affects them, improve their resiliency skills, identify community resources, and enhance family management. These interactive, student-centered lessons engage students as they develop resiliency skills and learn about community agencies. Suggested guest speakers on related topics are identified. Handouts are provided in English and Spanish. Learn more at www.streetlaw.org/content.asp?contentid=166.

Mock Elections—*Kids Voting USA* ® (www.kidsvotingusa.org) and *National Student/Parent Mock Election* (www.nationalmock election.org) help students explore the right to vote, participate in a democracy, and discover what it means to be an engaged citizen. In mock elections, millions of students cast their votes and express their positions on issues. Both programs offer paper and electronic voting. National and state results are announced. Ballots may replicate races and issues for each electoral district.

Youth Summits—Beginning in 1995, youth summits have been held annually to bring students together to discuss youth violence. The summits began through the efforts of the Office of Juvenile Justice and Delinquency Prevention to challenge students to become involved in their communities by offering them the opportunities to present solutions for problems facing those communities.

After studying contemporary and controversial problems, students come together and present their findings to policy makers. These experiences empower students by showing them how they can make a difference and have a positive influence on policy makers.

Youth for Justice has developed an extensive planning guide (www .crfc.org/pdf/ysguide.pdf) that contains a wealth of information on event planning, including formats for summits, program and partnership resources from the local community to the federal government, along with private and public organizations.

The American Bar Association also coordinates the National Online Youth Summit. Each year high school classes across the nation research and then discuss a public policy or related issue on message boards with other classes across the country. Topics vary annually. For more information, go to www.abanet.org/publiced/noys/home.html.

Model United Nations—Middle and high school students as well as college students participate in Model UN. Students role play ambassadors of member countries of the UN. Students learn rules of procedures and engage in caucusing, resolution writing, and public speaking as they study and present on global issues. Model UN exercises can be held in the classroom or in the school. Larger events that are regional, national, or international are called conferences. Topics vary at each UN simulation. You might want to see which UN-related organization is more active in the geographic area where you teach.

The United Nations Association of the United States (UNA-USA) holds an annual Summit and Leadership Conference where a variety of workshops are held. Planning and development support for teachers and preparation guides for students are also available at www.unausa.org/site/pp.asp?c=fvKRI8MPJpF&b=1081463.

Travel to Washington, D.C.—Whether you take your students on a formal civic education program such as Close Up's *Program for New Americans, Close Up Washington, D.C.,* (as an independent trip or in combination with Williamsburg, Philadelphia, or New York), or a private tour, there is nothing like a trip to the nation's capital. In the former, students prepare for visits to Capitol Hill with legislators and a view of the Supreme Court. They discuss the role of the media in society and debate current issues. Students begin to talk about domestic and foreign policy. Current events immediately become meaningful and personal. Students become interested in studying the law and public service. For more information on Close Up's middle school, high school, and teachers' programs, go to www.closeup.org. On both types of trips, students tour historic sites and monuments, go to museums, drive by the White House, and see the neighborhoods in the capital. They are amazed when they view in person the pictures they previously had seen only in their textbooks or on the Internet. You can easily find a tour or program that meets your needs. Connect with other teachers to become more aware of and informed about the planning and logistics. Many tours and programs offer pretour planning services and curricular materials. Some tours even offer continuing education units for teachers and high school credit for students.

EMPHASIZE ECONOMICS ACTIVITIES

Stock Market Game—As a fun way for students in Grades 4–12 to learn about our economic system, the Stock Market Game™ (SMG) is the only simulation game that has the endorsement of the National Council for Economic Education. With twenty years of experience, the Foundation for Investor Education, a nonprofit organization, annually involves over 700,000 students in the Stock Market Game. Students develop reading, math, and decision-making skills as they learn about saving and investing. Education and guidelines for teachers are available. The fees to participate vary by location; online, paper-based, and/or fax-based versions may be available in your area. Participating teachers receive monthly newsletters and curriculum materials along with support of state coordinators. It takes at least four sessions to introduce the game to students and time each week for students to trade, but the results are well worth the investment of time and energy. For more information, go to www.smgww.org/aboutsmg.htm. See if attendance in your classes improves as other teachers claim who use this activity with their students.

There are other stock market games too. Check with teachers and local brokerage firms in your geographic area for their support.

Economics Challenge—The Federal Reserve has a competition where high school students compete both individually and as teams. At the national finals, students are tested in four areas of economics: macroeconomics, microeconomics, current events/economic applications, and international economics; then the students participate as teams in a quiz bowl.

The National Economics Challenge competition is sponsored by the National Council on Economic Education (NCEE) and the Goldman Sachs Foundation. See http://economicschallenge.ncee.net. Teams of students from advanced placement and international baccalaureate classes along with honors students participate in the Adam Smith Division, while teams from single-semester (or less) general economics classes participate in the David Ricardo Division. Students are tested in the areas of microeconomics, macroeconomics, international economics, and current events via paper and pencil and oral quiz bowl formats. For team composition, student eligibility, rules, format, and coverage of travel expenses, see http://economicschallenge.ncee.net/rules.php. Winning state teams advance to the national competition.

Economic Simulations—Junior Achievement has developed JA Titan™, a microeconomic simulation for high school students. With a volunteer, students apply their knowledge of and experiences with economics to run a business in a fictional industry. Lesson plans and other supports are available. Junior Achievement has programs for elementary, middle, and high school students ranging from personal finance to running a business to economic investigations. See www.ja.org/programs/programs.shtml.

GENERATE GEOGRAPHY ACTIVITIES

National Geographic Bee—Students in public schools and home schools across the nation in Grades 4–8 study geography and participate in a competition known as the National Geographic Bee with materials prepared by the National Geographic Society. The purposes of the program are to encourage teachers to teach geography, to motivate students to study geography, and to promote public awareness of geography. Information on qualifying tests, school and state competitions, as well as school registration and student eligibility regulations and deadlines, can be found at www.nationalgeographic.com/geographybee/. Participating schools receive instructions, the questions booklet, and medals. The national competition is held in Washington, D.C., in May. National winners receive scholarships ranging from $10,000 to $25,000.

National Geography Awareness Week—Since 1987 when President Reagan signed a law establishing the third week of November as National Geography Awareness Week, the National Geographic Society has developed interdisciplinary geography materials for students of all ages. Each year is organized around a different theme with different contests and online quizzes. Many resources are available throughout the year, including Geokits and family geography activities. Plus, there are numerous summer institutes for teachers. Check out the teaching materials and professional development opportunities and grants for teachers at www.nationalgeographic.com/ education.

HIGHLIGHT HISTORY ACTIVITIES

National History Day—To engage students in studying primary source historical documents, use critical thinking, and actively engage in research, consider bringing National History Day to your classroom. National History Day (NHD) began when a history professor, Dr. David Van Tassel, from Case Western Reserve wanted to hold a contest for students to showcase their historical research. By 1980, the program had grown into National History Day. In 1992, the headquarters moved from Cleveland, Ohio, where it started, to Washington, D.C. The National Endowment for the Humanities and numerous other foundations and corporations support this program.

More than two million people—students, parents, teachers, and volunteers, are involved annually. Teacher support materials are available with workshops held regularly across the country. The national contest is held in June for students in Grades 6–12. Students can enter the contest on their own or as a group with up to five people. There are two divisions: junior (Grades 6–8) and senior (Grades 9–12). Following class, school, district, and region/county contests, state winners go on to the National History Day competition. Each year a different theme is presented for students to explore creatively as they design exhibits, organize documentaries, present performances, and/or write papers. Specific guidelines and more information can be found at www.nationalhistoryday.org.

Oral History—Beginning with the Foxfire Project in the 1960s, preserving oral histories has become a popular learning experience in social studies. Collecting oral histories is a way to have students use their skills actively and productively. This educational tool empowers students to record and present interviews that preserve an individual's history, while strengthening the students' own language skills. The Oral History Association has established appropriate goals, guidelines, and evaluation standards. Reference information is found at http://alpha.dickinson.edu/oha/.

Chautauquas—A special form of oral performance, chautauquas give students the opportunity to engage in historical investigation of a well-known figure and then portray that individual for an audience. Erb and Moore (2003) describe the steps. Students select a historical person to study; read and research the background of the figure; develop and present a first-person presentation incorporating costumes and props; and then answer questions from the audience, in a press conference format. Some teachers add an extra element of having students answer questions posing as the researcher. Teachers can assess the project at several points such as the note cards on the research, the oral presentation, and the knowledge on the historical figure. Parents love to come to class for these presentations! Students enjoy performing at assemblies for their peers.

Veterans History Project—Your students may want to participate in the Library of Congress Veterans History Project. Created in 2000 and supported by Congress, this project focuses on gathering narratives and documents, such as letters, diaries, and photographs, from veterans and civilians involved in various war efforts to preserve the stories and evidence of their experiences. Materials for interviewing and guidelines are available at www .loc.gov/vets.

State Resources—Many universities have oral history centers where you are likely to find materials. Another source of support may be your state historical society or state humanities council. As you collaborate with these organizations you may find grant opportunities for you and your students. There may be other projects in your state too. Once you begin your research and show interest, do not be surprised at the number of local volunteers who want to help you and join in your endeavors. Many local people are fascinated with the history of the area, particularly related to genealogy and their families, and will support your efforts in the classroom. Be sure to contact the local genealogical society too.

CONNECT TO CAREERS

Job Shadow Day—To encourage students to pursue careers related to social studies, take your students to visit a history museum curator or a geographer for a day. Materials and information on Job Shadow Day are available from www.jobshadow.org. This is a collaborative effort to have students see careers beyond what their parents do for a living. Students spend a day seeing a career that they might not otherwise see.

Coalition founders are America's Promise, Junior Achievement, the U.S. Department of Education, and the U.S. Department of Labor along with sponsoring agencies ING, Nelnet, and Valpak.com.

Your school or district also may have career day opportunities in which your students will either meet with representatives from different occupations and government services or travel to meet with professionals at their respective work sites. These are perfect times to collaborate with area universities and colleges too, so your students can understand why they need to earn specific degrees and apply for licenses to pursue some career goals. Most colleges and universities have recruiting departments with personnel who will be glad to help high school teachers and counselors make these connections for the students.

ENTER ESSAY CONTESTS

Each year a variety of essay contests for students are held that may appeal to your social studies students. Some contests are held at the local level; others at the state level; and many at the national level, with regional or state winners determined first. Most contests offer recognition; some contests will offer substantial prizes and/or trips to Washington, D.C., with a parent and teacher accompanying the state winner. Winning essays may be published.

Guidelines vary with respect to eligibility; most contests allow public, private, parochial, or home school students, but grades or age requirements differ. Children whose parents work for a sponsoring organization may not be eligible. Topics change yearly. Teachers often need to sign applications attesting to the ages and grades of participating students and the originality of their work. Guidelines for submission are frequently available online. Check the rules carefully. Note the maximum allowable word lengths and required formats. A sampling of opportunities follows.

- John F. Kennedy Library Foundation John F. Kennedy Profile in Courage Essay Contest: *www.jfkcontest.org*
- United States Institute of Peace National Peace Essay Contest: *www.usip.org/ed/npec/index.html*

- United Nations Association of the USA National High School Essay Contest: *www.unausa.org/site/pp .asp?c=fvKRI8 MPJpF&b=475725*

Professional organizations, federal and state government departments, and private organizations, such as the American Foreign Service; the Society of Professional Journalists High School Essay Contest; the Holland & Knight Charitable Foundation, Inc.'s Holocaust Remembrance Project; and the Elie Wiesel Foundation for Humanity also sponsor contests. Choose a topic that relates to your content standards and is suitable for your students. Students will see the merit of the writing skills they have been developing in their English and language arts classes. These types of essays also are excellent mechanisms for collaborating with other teachers in your school to integrate the curriculum.

DEVELOP SOCIAL STUDIES ACTIVITIES IN YOUR SCHOOL

There are many ways to incorporate school activities into your social studies classes. Students can contribute to the school newspaper; create a calendar or school map; participate in student council activities; and take leadership roles in school events.

School Newspaper—Many schools have newspapers. You could offer to take responsibility for a column or two focusing on social studies news and views along with social studies–related events on the school, community, state, national, or international scenes. Form student groups to write the reports and edit one another's work.

School E-mail List—Some schools have school-based e-mail distribution lists. Like the school newspaper, you could oversee a student committee to post news and social studies–related events.

School Calendar—Student groups could design a school calendar with all kinds of academic and social events illustrating each month. Again, here is an opportunity to demonstrate that social studies is part of everyday life.

School Map—What a great opportunity to incorporate local geography into your curriculum! You can organize your classes to draw a school map to be used with new students, guest speakers, parent volunteers, and so forth. Work with the school administrators and perhaps district personnel who have access to technological equipment that will enhance the final production. The map could be included with the school calendar too.

Student Council—Most schools have some form of student government. These structures encapsulate social studies firsthand as students understand, apply, and appreciate what government for the people and by the people actually means. Discuss elections for and actions taken by the student council with your students. You might want (or get) to be the school advisor.

School Store or Fund-Raising Events—If your school offers some type of school store, arrange for your students to see how it works from behind the counter. Invite the sponsors and students who operate the store to talk about the products, sales, profits, and so forth. The same suggestions apply when you hold school fund-raising events. You might want to volunteer to get your students involved so they experience economics firsthand.

Poster Contests—Offer to organize a poster contest for special days such as Safety Week in October, Healthy Heart Day in February, Earth Day in April, or other local events. Ask students to serve as the organizers, judges, and awards committees. They will enjoy participating in these types of functions.

School Plays and Concerts—Become involved with the school play. Most school plays convey an important historical as well as social message. This is the perfect opportunity to connect with a school-wide activity. The same applies to school musical presentations.

Debates—Your school may have a debate team and host debating contests. Usually specific topics are assigned. You could integrate your curriculum to coordinate with the topic and invite members of the debate team to share their skills with your social studies classes.

Parents' and Grandparents' Day—Almost all schools select a day to invite parents and/or grandparents to visit their schools. You can discuss all kinds of vocabulary and history related to parents, grandparents, and generational heritage. You can invite some parents and/or grandparents to talk with your class. This is great time to add to your resource bank too. (See Chapter 9.)

Elections—Many schools are designated voting locations. If you are fortunate enough to have elections held in your school, make arrangements for your students to see inside a voting booth. Take time to look at actual ballots, watch how voting occurs, talk with poll workers, listen to the exit polls, and so forth. This type of role modeling will impact your students forever in the democratic process.

CELEBRATE LEARNING THROUGH SOCIAL STUDIES

All school celebrations include aspects of social studies. Here are a few more ideas to consider:

Curriculum Fairs—Your school may create a fair in the spring for students to showcase their achievements. Students can construct displays that show various discussions, experiments, and discoveries. Capitalize on these opportunities to showcase social studies.

Awards Assemblies—Give out awards for your students' accomplishments. Honor those students who excel in social studies academically or by virtue of their participation and/or competition in programs, projects, and contests. Social studies needs to be celebrated just like sports, music, and other academics. Create your own awards; you can name the awards after exemplary alumni who graduated from your school.

Holidays and Cultural Events—These opportunities are all about social studies. Discuss the events the federal holidays commemorate. Note the cultural events in your community. Integrate your curriculum and instruction with other teachers to make the most of these memorable moments.

Dress-Up Day—Many schools hold dress-up days to show school spirit, in honor of a special historical event such as the State Day, and so forth. These days are ideal to showcase social studies in many different ways.

Book Displays and Book Talks—You might be fortunate enough to invite an author or illustrator to visit your school or to have book clubs. Showcase the books in your social studies class to connect the stories with your curriculum.

OFFER SERVICE LEARNING OPPORTUNITIES

Participants and recipients benefit from service learning projects. Students demonstrate their abilities as they take on responsibility for making a difference in their communities and meeting the real needs of its members. They like the sense that they are an appreciated and respected part of their community. They meet new and interesting people and have stories to tell as a result. Effective service learning requires careful planning, time for implementation, and time for reflection.

Active Citizenship—For a variety of citizenship-related activities, such as persuasive writing, public speaking, developing posters, campaigning, and utilizing community resources, *Active Citizenship Today* (second edition) is appropriate for middle and high school students. This guide provides a step-by-step approach for conducting service learning projects. Students explore problems, analyze policy, develop potential solutions, create and implement an action plan, and evaluate its progress. This is a joint project of the Close Up Foundation and the Constitutional Rights Foundation. For more information see www.crf-usa.org/information.html.

Youth Courts—As a way to give students ages eight to eighteen opportunities to practice the skills they are learning in the classroom, youth courts, also known as teen courts, are gaining popularity across the country. After being informed of the principles and procedures of our judicial system, participants deliver justice to first-time youth offenders or youth with problem behaviors—with their parents' permission—who would otherwise appear before the court. Students learn about the legal process and work with adult mentors, filling the roles of attorney, judge, community advocate, juror, bailiff, or clerk depending on the structure of the particular program. There are many guides available for teachers. The National Youth Court Center serves as a clearinghouse and offers workshops. See www.youthcourt.net.

Students in Service to America—The National Service Learning Clearinghouse offers tools and resources for K–12 teachers to begin service learning projects in their classrooms. Information on After School Programs, Youth Leadership Clubs and Organizations, and Recognition Programs are linked to their Web site at www .studentsinservicetoamerica.org/guidebook/tools.html.

CityYouth: Today's Communities—Designed for middle school teachers, this Constitutional Rights Foundation program can be used in the classroom or as an afterschool activity. It has thirty-two lessons organized around four themes: Crime and Safety, Harmony, Health and Well-Being, and Environment. Students apply concepts they learn to service learning projects and evaluate them.

CityWorks—Designed for Grades 9–12, *CityWorks* (published by the Constitutional Rights Foundation) has students participating as citizens in a simulated city, learning about local government and city policies and engaging in a service learning project.

Take Charge: A Youth Guide to Community Change—This Constitutional Rights Foundation publication is geared for Grades 8–12 with a focus on creating positive community change. Students not only learn about their communities, they get involved in organizing and implementing a project that gives them responsibility and ownership.

SPONSOR A CLUB

From a former high school teacher: *"The Foreign Exchange Club was one of the most popular clubs at my school. Each year the school would host at least two students from different countries. Our club provided an opportunity for our students to get to know the visitors and a place for the visitors to share a little about their culture and make friends. We built a float for Homecoming, sponsored a school dance, and hosted a table for future members at the Club Fair. You really get to know another side of your students through club participation."*

Sponsoring a club is a great way to spend time with students outside the classroom. Away from the classroom, you take on a different role serving as a resource person helping students achieve their goals. As a club advisor you will be involved with students over many years, rather than just a semester or year, and you will be able to watch them grow and develop into mature adolescents as they take on positions of leadership and pursue their interests.

Many organizations have brochures and toolkits for teachers to get started. They contain suggestions for planning events, conducting activities, and promoting the group. Information on holding events with background information can be found on their Web sites along with sample forms and other documents. Resource materials can be found online and in print.

Look in your school's student handbook or ask your department chair about social studies clubs and organizations. The clubs may be looking for an advisor or additional advisors. Or you might want to start a club. Most schools have established days and times for clubs to meet at school. Some clubs meet before school, some meet at lunch, some meet after school. Table 11.1 has a sampling of social studies-related clubs:

Table 11.1   Social Studies-Related Clubs

Amnesty International	Junior Statesmen
Biography Book Club	Mock Trial
Civil War Reenactment	Model Congress
Cultural (based on ethnicity and nationality)	Model United Nations
Current Events	Multicultural
Debate	National History Day
Economics	Philosophy
Fed Challenge	Politics and Policy
Geography	Service
Geography Bee	Social Studies
Geography Information Systems (GIS)	Social Studies Quiz Bowl or Quiz Team
Habitat for Humanity	Social Studies Software
History	Student Council
International	*We the People: Project Citizen*
Junior Achievement	*We the People: The Citizen and the Constitution*

Have Fun With Social Studies . . .

You have many choices for making social studies real and exciting. As you grow personally, pedagogically, and professionally, your efforts will make a huge difference for your students and for you. Everyone will be more engaged and energized when you incorporate special activities into your social studies courses. In our final chapter, we look at ways to reflect on your practice and offer our secrets for further professional development.

Suggested Activities

1. Talk with your social studies colleagues about service learning in your community. Explore how they got involved and how their students benefit.

2. Find one special activity to incorporate into your social studies courses. Plan how and when you will introduce it to your students.

3. Visit another school to see the kinds of social studies clubs that are available. Talk with the advisors.

4. Research professional development opportunities, including summer institutes, in your area.

CHAPTER TWELVE

Reflect on Your Practices *to Prepare for the Future*

You have your entire teaching career stretching out in front of you. The secret is to start by taking an honest inventory of your own knowledge, skills, and dispositions. Assess your competence, confidence, and readiness related to all of your responsibilities as well as your aspirations. Set some realistic goals and then take the essential steps to put your goals into motion. Enjoy the journey. And be sure to pace yourself. Your goals may be ambitious and you don't want to burn out. The secret is to balance what you think you need to do with want you want to do. Our advice for you is exactly the advice you would give to your students.

LOOK BACK TO LOOK AHEAD

The first step in looking ahead requires you to look back and reflect on your teaching (Schön, 1983). Take stock of what you know, do, and believe about social studies content and pedagogy. Consider what you value most as you establish your learning communities and identify the next steps that will benefit both you and your students (Van Manen, 1977). It is important to reflect on what worked and what did not work when you were a learner in the very same grade level and/or classes where you are now the teacher. Then reflect on what works and does not work now for your students in a contemporary context (Ziechner & Liston, 1987).

REFLECT ON LEARNING WITH PURPOSE

Becoming a reflective practitioner is vital to advancing your professionalism throughout your teaching career (Pultorak, 1993). Many teachers take time at the end of each day to mentally review the day. We encourage you to make some notes on your lesson plans or to keep a journal. You may want to talk with colleagues. Whatever format or combination you follow, we find adding structure will enhance your experience.

Hole and McEntee (1999) developed the Guided Reflection Protocol to help individual teachers improve their teaching by responding to four prompts. First the teacher describes an experience by writing about it in a concentrated manner. Writing helps to clarify and personalize one's ideas. Then the teacher seeks an explanation and adds that to the narrative. Next, an attempt is made to discover the significance, and finally, the teacher determines future action in light of this analysis extending the narrative with each additional insight. Here are the four prompts or questions as found in the Guided Reflection Protocol:

1. What happened?

2. Why did it happen?

3. What might it mean?

4. What are the implications for my practice?

Jonson (2002) suggests that reflective thinking is most powerful when teachers talk to one another about their ideas. It is helpful to have an active listener respond to your description and share in your evaluation in a way that will promote your personal growth. Talking with a colleague can be very supportive.

Hole and McEntee (1999) also developed a structure to use with others in a group process experience. This is called the Critical Incidents Protocol. Each teacher in the group takes time to write an account; then the members share their accounts. The group chooses one account on which to focus its conversation. The author reads what he or she has written and then answers "clarifying questions" posed by the group such as:

1. What does this account mean within the larger context of your life?

2. What metaphors stand out in the account that represent important themes to you?

3. What are some alternative endings for the account that you considered plausible?

4. What are some alternative endings for the account that you rejected?

5. What does this account reveal about your teaching that you value most?

Such questions lead to a deeper discussion of the issues raised in the account, not only for the author, but also for the other members of the group. Participants then have the opportunity to personalize the themes and discuss the implications for their own practices, and the group debriefs the process.

From a first-year social studies teacher: "*I felt I was not closing my classes effectively. My tendency was to cram too much into the class period and race through the discussion so I would be sure to collect papers before the period ended.*

"*I joined a group of first-year teachers after school one afternoon just for fun and we found ourselves reflecting on the day. Another teacher mentioned closure as a challenge so I shared my similar experiences. We began to brainstorm ideas to try, like posting agendas and using timers and having students complete exit cards and journal activities. We decided to meet the following week to report on our individual progress. I felt safe with the other first-year teachers and greatly appreciated both their ideas and support. I focused on closing class more effectively so I could share my success with the other teachers. I even started writing down my strengths and weaknesses so I could make more improvements.*"

Whether conducted individually, with a partner, or in a group, reflection gives you the opportunity to explore in detail the results of your decisions—what went well and why, as well as what needs improvement. Whether you take time daily, weekly, or biweekly, reflection allows you to analyze past events, acknowledging your accomplishments supporting the development of your teaching skills and the successes of your students (Shermis, 1992). You also identify and learn from mistakes in order to change what you will do in the future. Perhaps you need to clarify directions, change the sequence of activities, or provide additional background for students in a unit of learning. In talking with others, you may get new ideas, strategies, and resources to try. You may choose to observe the way other master teachers address the same concept or skill or decide to pursue some other professional development.

EVALUATE YOUR CURRICULUM

Beyond looking at lessons, effective teachers examine their curriculum as a whole. We have developed a tool for this type of reflection, which looks at your teaching and the respective student learning in four categories. On a broader level, you will evaluate the extent to which authentic learning, academic focus, active learning, and alternative assessments take place in your classroom. In Resource E you will find the Social Studies Curriculum Evaluation Tool.

As you determine what your needs are as a teacher, you will find many people and opportunities to promote your efforts to change your practice or do things differently in the future. We hope we have been helpful as we shared some of our experiences and observations throughout this book. While we have tried to provide a wide variety of ideas, our suggestions are by no means comprehensive nor do we mean them to be prescriptive. We know you will continue to add to your repertoire as you personalize the text for your own use. Below we look at the benefits of joining professional organizations, finding a mentor, traveling, and pursuing further education for your professional growth.

JOIN PROFESSIONAL ORGANIZATIONS

By joining professional organizations, you will be able to keep up with the latest developments in the field and to network with other teachers who share your interests. Your membership will provide you with journals publishing research and best practices along with other notices of conferences, meetings, and special events.

Membership also entitles you to reduced rates to attend conferences and order additional materials. We strongly encourage you to join different professional organizations as a way to get involved and to stay informed.

The main organization related to social studies is the National Council for the Social Studies (NCSS): www.ncss.org. This is an organization composed of K–12 classroom teachers, department chairs, curriculum specialists, and university professors interested in and representing the associated groups of social studies education. Once you are a member, you will have access to the entire Web site. The newsletter, *The Social Studies Professional (TSSP)* will keep you abreast of meetings, conferences, programs for students, and educational activities for teachers and administrators. Other publications provide theoretical content, teaching ideas, lesson plans, and innovative updates on technology for teachers at various grade levels. NCSS also publishes curriculum standards, books, and bulletins.

Each state has a chapter of NCSS. Look on the NCSS Web site for links to your state. Most of the state chapters hold annual conferences and meetings in various locations around the state. Join a state chapter of NCSS to network with other social studies professionals near you and to find out more about the content resources in your state. And, fortunately, most state social studies chapters offer a comprehensive membership so you can join the national and state councils all at once.

There are organizations in all of the social studies–related academic disciplines. Many national professional organizations have active state and local chapters as well, such as Geographic Alliances. Even if you cannot attend meetings or conferences, becoming a member will entitle you to receive their journals or newsletters with academic research and classroom practices, discounts on additional publications, announcements related to the subject area, such as newsworthy events and television specials, opportunities to apply for classroom grants, and a preview of future activities. Here are some organizations and their Web site addresses for civics, economics, geography, history, and humanities.

Civics

National Alliance for Civic Education (NACE)—Advances civic knowledge and engagement: www.cived.net

Economics

National Council on Economic Education (NCEE)—Promotes economic literacy with students and their teachers: www.ncee.net

Geography

Association of American Geographers (AAG)—Supports the theory, methods, and practice of geography: www.aag.org/Info/info.html

National Council for Geographic Education (NCGE)—Enhances the status and quality of geography teaching and learning: www.ncge.org

Geography Alliance Network—Improves geography education supported by the National Geographic Society Education Foundation: http://ngsednet.org/community/about.cfm?community_id=94

National Geographic Society—Increases and diffuses geographic knowledge in ways that inspire people to care about the planet: www.nationalgeographic.com

History

American Historical Association (AHA)—Promotes historical studies, the collection and preservation of historical documents and disseminates research; cosponsors National History Day (see Chapter 11): www.historians.org/index.cfm

National Council for History Education (NCHE)—Promotes the importance of history in schools and in society: www.garlandind.com/nche

Humanities

National Endowment for the Humanities (NEH)—Supports research, education, preservation, and public programs in the humanities: www.neh.gov

You may discover that a conference will be held in or near your school that you can attend through advance arrangements with your department chair, principal, and/or district curriculum specialist. You may be able to receive financial assistance to attend the conference if you submit a proposal to present your own action research and/or teaching practices. Some districts may request you lead a workshop when you return to share what you learned at the conference with other teachers. Presentations are excellent opportunities to collaborate with your colleagues too.

GO TO A SOCIAL STUDIES CONFERENCE

Attending a conference is a unique experience. Depending on where you live, social studies–related conferences may be held independently or connected with general teacher education conferences. Held at the national, state, and local levels, you will be able to immerse yourself in social studies conversations, see the latest textbooks and newest supplementary materials, talk to resource professionals, gain knowledge of current pedagogy, and view the latest technology.

The secret is to wisely select the sessions you attend, according to your needs and interests. Look for special interest strands in the conference program. Note the featured speakers. Plan to spend time visiting exhibits. There will be opportunities for you to be a presenter and share your research and/or students' accomplishments too. You will meet new people, learn what other teachers are doing in their classrooms, and come home inspired.

From a new teacher: *"As a world history teacher I needed activities to engage my struggling readers. At my first state conference I saw a wonderful Interact simulation. I tried it with immediate success in my classroom. Now, I go to state and national conferences every year searching for more ideas. I even presented my students' work at a state conference."*

FIND A MENTOR

All of us were new to our positions at one time, and we quickly appreciated the mentoring we received as teacher candidates from our cooperating/master teacher(s) and university supervisor(s). Hopefully, you have a mentor who is current in and enthusiastic about the research and practice of teaching as well as mentoring (Portnor, 2002). If you have not been assigned to a mentor, you can either request one from your department chair or ask a school administrator to identify a person to fulfill that role for you. Or, you can ask an experienced social studies colleague to serve informally as your mentor. Most experienced teachers will be honored to support you.

Many states have formal programs to ensure that new teachers and teachers new to their positions receive the assistance and guidance they need to be successful (Jonson, 2002). In fact, many school districts now have formalized induction programs that include orientations and programs for new teachers where mentors are assigned and time is allocated to delve into a variety of issues and concerns. Meetings are held on a regular basis (sometimes weekly, biweekly, or monthly) for new teachers to assemble, to listen to a speaker address a timely topic or important issue, to interact with other new teachers, and to provide one another much-needed support. These sessions are led by experienced teachers who have received professional development to provide support. They guide the sessions in positive and productive ways. Typical topics and issues include time management, classroom management, authentic assessments, standardized testing, teaching strategies, and lesson review. Some university credit may be available for participation in beginning teacher and induction programs.

From a new teacher: "*My Support Provider helped me tremendously! He gave me guidance, but also allowed me to experiment with new techniques and strategies without being critical. I appreciated the freedom and support that he gave me! My Support Provider also taught me invaluable reflection methods that I use when evaluating lessons and/or assignments. He was a BIG help particularly with one of my economics lessons.*

"*I knew that middle school students were not excited about economics. I think just the word scares them off. My Support Provider showed me the Consumer Price Index Web site. You can go onto this site to compare and contrast today's prices of items with the prices from another specific year. My students were fascinated. They could not wait to check out the prices of their possessions and tell their parents. Then my students told me how their parents wanted to be shown the Web site. One student reported that his grandfather was refinishing a car, a 1937 REO Wagon. The grandfather checked out the original price of his car with the price he had paid.*

"*Later when I was reflecting on this lesson, my Support Provider told me that I had expanded upon the economics lesson in ways that he had never imagined. We talked about more ways to expand the lesson in the future. My Support Provider suggested I record my ideas in a journal."*

ATTEND A CLASS, WORKSHOP, OR INSTITUTE

After you begin teaching, you will discover how much more you want to know and be able to do. From a new teacher: *"Shortly after the school year began, I was asked to teach a comparative governments class in the spring. I realized that I needed more background, so I immediately contacted the university and found a class. Ironically, this is how I started my master's degree. During this course it dawned on me that I should take one course a semester to build upon my undergraduate degree, to expand my opportunities at the high school where I taught, and to move up on the pay scale."*

Most universities offer programs of study designed to match your career goals and special interests. You might want to earn an additional endorsement on your credential, a master's degree, an education specialist degree, or even a doctorate. Why not take classes that you not only want to take but will possibly open some future doors for you too? Look at the Web site for the university department where you are interested in taking classes or contact the department chair to start your exploration.

One unique program, designed especially for social studies teachers, is the James Madison Fellowships. This program offers senior fellowships to U.S. citizens or nationals who teach or plan to teach American history, American government, or social studies in Grades 7–12 to complete their degrees. Learn more about requirements, obligations, and awards at www.jamesmadison.com.

Summer institutes are very popular. They run from one or two weeks up to a month and are offered by a variety of discipline-based as well as education-related organizations, including the National Endowment for the Humanities (www.neh.gov/projects/si-school.html). Programs are also offered by school, county, regional, or intermediate districts. Check for the application deadlines, eligibility, and availability of fellowship programs and stipends. You may also qualify for university credit or professional development units from your school district.

LOOK AT SOCIAL STUDIES LITERATURE

There are several journals to support social studies teachers specifically, such as NCSS' *Social Studies and the Young Learner, Middle Level Learning, Social Education;* Heldref Publications' *The Social Studies;* and The University of Alabama's electronic *Social Studies and Research Practice.* These peer-reviewed journals offer teacher-tested classroom lessons, current research developments in the field, links with literacy, and ideas for integrating the latest technology in the classroom. There are also publications in the academic disciplines.

In both university and commercial bookstores you will find books related to teaching strategies that will appeal to your students' interests. If you like presenting mysteries, consider *Creative Ways to Teach the Mysteries of History* (Pahl, 2005) or *Economics and the Environment: Eco-Detectives* (Schug, Morton, & Wentworth, 1999). You may need to look at materials earmarked as "elementary" or "secondary" education; many of those materials will fit your social studies classes quite well. You can consider adapting social studies strategies for one level to fit the other.

TRAVEL TO BROADEN YOUR PERSPECTIVE

Going to a new place is a wonderful source of personal inspiration, and educational growth, especially for social studies teachers. Sometimes you can travel as part of a study group either through application and selectivity or simply by signing up and going along. Organized tours allow you to meet and network with other educators who can share all kinds of ideas with you. The organized tours usually provide you with opportunities to see things or do things that most tourists would not have the chance to see and do.

Educational tours might be organized around a selected theme, topic, or issue. Perhaps you want to go on a particular kind of tour examining art and architecture, contemporary culture, history and museums, battlegrounds and war. Your tour may be work-related as in helping people, relocating animals, digging for fossils, saving the environment, promoting democracy, and so forth. The choices for travel are limitless.

Another opportunity for travel is with The Fulbright-Hays Group Projects Abroad Programs. These projects enable teachers to visit another country for five to six weeks to study a culture or an area of a culture and acquire resource materials for curriculum development. Currently, Fulbright-Hays projects must focus on the following countries: Africa, East Asia, South Asia, Southeast Asia and the Pacific, the Western Hemisphere (Central and South America, Mexico, and the Caribbean), East Central Europe and Eurasia, and the Near East. Information is available at www.ed.gov/programs/iegpsgpa/index.html.

From a Fulbright participant: "*After we returned from our trip to Thailand, not only were we able to describe cultural practices, we were able to model them. We brought back a variety of artifacts, including children's toys, musical instruments, art, crafts, religious items, and clothing. We bought documentary videos, books, posters, and CDs of current and traditional music. Students can now have a sensory, three-dimensional experience, providing a better understanding of the lives of the Thai people.*"

And many of you will want to take your own individual trips, both short and long, to see the world, near and far. Keep your classes and students in mind as your travel so you can collect artifacts to use as reference, to display, and to give away. Many travel sites have educational centers or gift shops with information that you can have for free or purchase at reduced prices when you tell them you are a teacher. Be sure to take your school district identification card with you.

Some school districts will allow teachers to earn professional development credits if you join an approved travel program. Investigate the expectations carefully. You may be required to submit your itinerary to the district or state to confirm your trip long in advance of your anticipated travels. You also may be required to give a report on how you were able to use what you learned in your classroom or conduct a presentation for other teachers on what you learned to earn your credits.

Travel is the best way for you to learn more about the cultures you are teaching and more about yourself. From your travels, you will be able to speak with genuine knowledge and understanding of all kinds of people and their cultures. Likely, you will bring back many artifacts and photographs to share with your students.

KEEP AN OPEN AND ACTIVE MIND

You give your students ownership of their learning when you stay open and active yourself. New events and ideas are going to come along everyday. That is the very nature of social studies. Social studies is contemporary and dynamic. The new events and ideas may confirm or conflict with your thoughts and beliefs or the accepted thoughts and beliefs in your geographic region. These insights and interactions also are essential aspects of social studies. We strongly encourage you to be alert to change and continue your own learning along with your students.

What and how you teach now will not be the same throughout your teaching career. New discoveries will be made, and new resources developed. With each new political administration, you can anticipate a change in focus that will become part of your state, school, and classroom. The changes will require time for implementation.

When you get involved at your school, in your school district, and at the state level of education, you become a part of the future of education. You teach about being in a participatory citizenship, so you want to apply this principle in your own profession. You will be amazed at the rewards you reap when you get involved. You will know that you have played a vital role in the future of education whether it is voting on textbook adoptions, developing curriculum, refining academic standards, creating instructional materials, or participating in some other educational activity. Your contributions will be welcomed.

Become the Teacher You Always Wanted to Be . . .

Deep inside you is the teacher you always wanted to be. Now is the time to fulfill those plans. There are many different kinds of teacher knowledge (Shulman, 1987) that you will develop throughout your career. We leave you with these final secrets to success:

Share your personal history. Talk about your past experiences. Your students want to hear about you. Share the discoveries you've made that will help them to become inquisitive learners and solid citizens. Sharing about yourself will be inspiration to both your students and to you.

Act spontaneously. Take some risks to enrich your life and enhance your teaching. When you learn more about the world, you learn more about yourself and have more to offer your students. Teaching is both a journey *and* a destination.

Teach in the moment. Life *is* social studies so teach about it when it happens. Events may occur in the school or community, across the country, or around the world that you will want to bring into your classroom *as* they happen. Stay alert and try not to miss these teachable moments.

Build reserves. Take care of yourself so you are competent, confident, and ready both in and out of the classroom as you pace yourself through the school year. You want to be healthy and hearty in mind, body, and spirit.

Consider your dreams and desires realistically. Set goals and identify the steps and resources you need and want to reach them. Dreams are fulfilled by chance and by choice. Celebrate successes along the way.

You WILL become the social studies teacher you always wanted to be. Best wishes for success in your classroom!

Resources

Resource A—
Social Studies Textbook
Evaluation Tool

Rate each item based on a score of "5" to "1" with "5" being high and "1" being low. Mark "0" for items not observed. Space is provided at the end for additional notes.

ITEM	RATING and COMMENT 5 high; 1 low; 0 not observed
Overall Organization	
Coverage of State-Specific Standards	
Visually Appealing Layout	
Integration of Primary Resources	
Diversity of People's Contributions	
Multiple Perspectives	
Diversity of People in Photographs	
Connections to Students' Lives	
Historical Interpretation Skills	
Chronological/Spatial Skills	
Research/Evidence/Point of View Skills	
Variety of Activities	

ITEM	RATING and COMMENT *5 high; 1 low; 0 not observed*
Clarity of Maps (with appropriate titles)	
Graphs and Pictorial Representations	
Chapter Overviews	
Headings to Divide Sections	
Variety of Assessments	
Rich Narrative	
Key Terms Highlighted	
Definitions or Context Cues for Difficult Words	
Controlled Vocabulary	
End-of-Chapter Summaries	
Technology Extensions	
Glossary	
Index	
OVERALL RATING	

ADDITIONAL NOTES:

Resource B— Sample Social Studies Concepts by Level

UPPER ELEMENTARY MIDDLE LEVEL	MIDDLE SCHOOL JUNIOR HIGH SCHOOL	HIGH SCHOOL
CIVICS/CITIZENSHIP		
Authority	Campaigns	Bureaucracy
Citizens' Responsibilities	Civic Procedures	Civic Courts
Conflict and Cooperation	Common Good	Conduct of Citizens
Constitutional Rights	Constitution	Core Democratic Values
Core Democratic Values	Criminal Procedures	Criminal Courts
Decisions	Domestic Policy	Diversity in U.S. Life
Declaration of Independence	Forms of Government	Federal System
Freedom	Individual Rights	Foreign Policy
Government, Branches of	International Governments	Parliamentary Systems
Influence	Laws (Making, Enforcing, and Interpreting)	Political Behaviors
International Events	Monarchy	Practices of Government
Justice	Representative Democracy	U.S. Influences on Other Countries

UPPER ELEMENTARY MIDDLE LEVEL	MIDDLE SCHOOL JUNIOR HIGH SCHOOL	HIGH SCHOOL
National Events	State, Local, and National Governments	U.S. Political System
Rules	State and Federal Courts	U.S. Presidential System
ECONOMICS		
Business	Assets	Capitalism
Cash	Barter	Domestic Economy
Commerce	Benefits	Economic Growth
Consumer	Capital	Economic Indicators
Currency	Credit	Enterprise
Distribution	Corporation	Fiscal Policy
Earning	Cost	Foreign Market Economy
Goods	Decision-Making Model	Free Market Economy
Market Economy	Demand	Inflation
Partnership	Entrepreneur	Interest
Production	Export	Investment
Price	Import	International Economic System
Private Goods	Incentives	Marketplace
Public Goods	Individual Ownership	Materialism
Resources	Natural Resources	Portfolio
Risks	Opportunity Cost	Private Equity
Savings	Stock Market	Quota
Services	Supply	Specialization
Scarcity	Public Goods	Tariff
Trade	Taxes	Securities

UPPER ELEMENTARY MIDDLE LEVEL	MIDDLE SCHOOL JUNIOR HIGH SCHOOL	HIGH SCHOOL
GEOGRAPHY		
Boundaries	Adaptations	Cultural Stability and Change
Community	Communication	Economic Development
Continent	Cultural Geography	Global Communication
Country	Cross-cultural Relations	International Trade
Culture	Geography	Perceptions
Environment	Ecosystems	Political Systems
Location	Human Geography	Population Growth
Major World Event	Land Use	Processes
Movement	Migration	Use of Resources
Ocean	Occupation	World Events
Resources	Patterns	World Patterns
Transportation	Transportation	World Processes
Time Zones	World Regions	Urbanization
HISTORY		
Autobiography	Contemporary Life	Allies
Biography	Context	Change Over Time
Chronological Order	Century	Cold War
Facts	Decade	Contemporary Factors
Family History	Defense	Global Impact
Interpretation	Defining Characteristic	Historical Analogies
Narrative	Historical Biographies	Inevitability

UPPER ELEMENTARY MIDDLE LEVEL	MIDDLE SCHOOL JUNIOR HIGH SCHOOL	HIGH SCHOOL
Opinion	Historical Eras	Key or Pivotal Decisions
Past, Present, and Future	Historical Origins	Leadership
Patterns	International Relations	Nationalism
Personal History	Key Events	Personal Virtue
Point of View	Primary Sources	Platform
Primary Documents	Secondary Sources	Tiered Time Lines
Records of the Past	Sequence	War
Time Line	Treaty	Weaponary
Weeks, Months, Years	World Citizenship	World Peace

GENERAL SOCIAL STUDIES
(At all grade levels as developmentally appropriate)

Belief Systems	Equity	Power
Challenge	Expansion	Production
Change	Financial Institutions	Reasoning
Choice	Foreign Trade	Recession
Civic Responsibility	Freedom	Reconstruction
Civic Values	Free Markets	Reform
Civil War Citizenship	Geographic Systems	Regions
Civilization	Globalization	Relationships
Colonization	Governmental Systems	Religion
Communication	Human Systems	Responsibilities
Consumption	Human Rights	Revolution
Contemporary	Identity	Rights
Culture	Imperialism	Roles
Decision making	Industrialization	Scarcity
Democracy	Interdependence	Science
Depression	Justice	Settlement
Distribution	Labor	Technology
Diversity	Movement	Trade
Hemisphere	Nation-State	Time Zones
Economic Systems	Nationalism	Transportation
Elections	Native Americans	Urbanization
Empathy	Needs and Wants	Values
Empires	Physical Systems	Voting
Enterprise	Places	War
Environment	Political System	World in Spatial Terms

Resource C— Detailed Lesson Plan Guide

Lesson Plan Guide (Detailed)	
1. Title of Lesson	Catchy name that describes the desired knowledge, skills, and dispositions
2. Goals	General outcomes that students will have at the end of the lesson, unit, and school year; goals frequently align with the unit themes and national and state standards
3. Objectives	Specific outcomes that students will demonstrate at the end of the lesson; usually stated as, "The learner will . . . "; objectives frequently align with the unit topic issues and district scope and sequence academic expectations
4. Inquiry Question	Prompt to help you set the tone and begin the learning; models an investigative approach that is curious and constructivist

5. Preparation	Detailed descriptions of:
	a) Schema activation
	b) Supplies and materials
	c) Time and space
	d) Anticipatory set and motivation
	e) Accommodations and modifications for:
	    (1) English language learners
	    (2) gifted and talented students
	    (3) special education students
	    (4) individual instruction of any kind
	f) Connections to life, living, and the community

6. Procedures	Steps for completing this lesson; usually procedures are stated as "The teacher will . . . " balanced with "The student will . . . " Be sure to include concrete examples, yet allow for individual expression regarding learning and outcomes
7. Integration	Ideas for connecting this particular learning experience with language arts, math, science, social studies, health, technology, and fine arts
8. Vocabulary	Key words to emphasize during this learning experience, including academic with content words and terms
9. Guided Practice	Activities that students complete in class with the guidance of the teacher so the teacher can ensure that all students understand expectations
10. Independent Practice	Activities that students complete either independently in class or outside of class to practice and apply the new learning
11. Closure	Revisiting and recapping the highlights of the learning processes and lesson outcomes with students at the end of the lesson
12. Assessments	Performance-based demonstrations showing mastery of the objectives
13. Evaluation	Reflection on the effectiveness of the overall learning experience, outcomes, and teaching

Resource D—Abbreviated Lesson Plan Guide

Lesson Plan Guide (Abbreviated)	
1. Objectives	1. The learner will . . .
2. Standards	2. To fulfill . . .
3. Preparations	3. Using . . .
4. Introduction	4. By connecting with . . .
5. Body of Lesson	5. Through the following activities . . .
6. Closure	6. Summarized by . . .
7. Assessments	7. Demonstrated by . . .
8. Evaluation and Reflection	8. Next time, I will . . .

Resource E— Social Studies Curriculum Evaluation Tool

To what extent do you implement authentic learning, maintain an academic focus, involve students in active learning, and provide articulated assessment? Always? Sometimes? Not yet? For each of these categories, there are four questions for you to answer in this self-diagnostic tool.

AUTHENTIC LEARNING

To what extent do teaching and learning . . .	Always	Sometimes	Not Yet
• Emanate from a problem or question that has meaning to the learner and implications for humanity?			
• Provide opportunities to create or produce a product or outcome that has personal and social value?			
• Provide opportunities to integrate content, processes, and context while working within a variety of cooperative learning groups?			
• Extend to a real audience and genuine effect?			

ACADEMIC FOCUS

To what extent do teaching and learning . . .	*Always*	*Sometimes*	*Not Yet*
• Guide learners in acquiring, applying, and appreciating one or more social studies disciplines or content areas?			
• Model and reinforce understanding and developing skills using critical thinking, decision making, and problem solving?			
• Support learners in establishing habits of mind as well as work required to complete complex tasks and to be resourceful?			
• Challenge students to learn new concepts and practices with a variety of resources and technology?			

ACTIVE LEARNING

To what extent do teaching and learning . . .	*Always*	*Sometimes*	*Not Yet*
• Dedicate significant amounts of time to conduct field-based work to complete products and outcomes?			
• Challenge learners to build upon their individual learning styles and strengths while nurturing weaker areas?			
• Include real investigations and use a variety of methods, media, and sources during the investigations?			
• Connect classroom experiences with the community in ways that are positive and useful?			

ARTICULATED ASSESSMENT

To what extent do teaching and learning . . .	Always	Sometimes	Not Yet
• Align assessments with educational objectives?			
• Involve participation by both teacher and learner in setting the criteria related to the processes, products, and outcomes?			
• Expect reflection by both teacher and learner relative to the processes, products, and outcomes?			
• Provide for learners to demonstrate their achievement in a variety of ways?			

Reflect on your practices noting the area(s) you feel need strengthening . . .	Develop an action plan that identifies . . .		
	Specific Objectives	Applicable Resources	Time Lime
1.			
2.			
3.			

Readings and References

Ainsworth, L. (2003). *Power standards: Identifying the standards that matter most.* Englewood, CO: Advanced Learning Press.

Alleman, J., & Brophy, J. (1993). Is curriculum integration a boon or a threat to social studies? *Social Education, 57*(6), 287–291.

Armstrong, T. (1994). *Multiple intelligences in the classroom.* Alexandria, VA: Association for Supervision and Curriculum Development.

Ausubel, D. P. (1963). *The psychology of meaningful learning.* New York: Grune & Stratton.

Barr, R. D., Barth, J. L., & Shermis, S. S. (1978). *The nature of social studies.* Palm Springs, CA: ETC (Education Technology Communication) Publications.

Beyer, B. K. (1995). *Critical thinking.* Bloomington, IN: Phi Delta Kappa Educational Foundation.

Bloom, B. (1984). *Taxonomy of educational objectives, book 1.*White Plains, NY: Longman.

Bol, L., & Strange, A. (1996). The contradiction between teachers' instructional goals and their assessment practices in high school biology courses. *Science Education, 80*(2), 145–163.

Borich, G. D., & Tombari, M. L. (2003). *Educational assessment for the elementary and middle school classroom* (2nd ed.). Upper Saddle River, NJ: Pearson Education.

Brogan, B. R., & Brogan, W. A. (1995). The Socratic questioner: Teaching and learning in a dialogical classroom. *Educational Forum, 59*(3), 288–296.

Brooks, J. G., & Brooks, M. G. (1999). *In search of understanding: The case for constructivist classrooms.* Englewood Cliffs, NJ: Prentice-Hall.

Brophy, J., & Alleman, J. (1996). *Powerful social studies for elementary students.* Fort Worth, TX: Harcourt Brace & Company.

Brunner, J. (1959). *The process of education.* Cambridge, MA: Harvard University Press.

California International Studies Project. (n.d.). *Historical and social studies analysis skills.* Retrieved June 28, 2006, from http://csmp.ucop.edu/cisp/standards/historical.html

Callahan, J. F., Clark, L. H., & Kellough, R. D. (1998). *Teaching in the middle and secondary schools* (6th ed.). Upper Saddle River, NJ: Prentice Hall.

Carmine, L., & Carmine, D. (2004). The interaction of reading skills and science content knowledge when teaching struggling secondary students. *Reading & Writing Quarterly, 20*(2), 203–218.

Cattani, D. H. (2002). *A classroom of her own: How new teachers develop instructional, professional, and cultural competence.* Thousand Oaks, CA: Corwin Press.

Costa, A. (1991). The inquiry strategy. In A. Costa (Ed.), *Developing minds: A resource book for teaching* (pp. 302–303). Alexandria, VA: Association for Supervision and Curriculum Development.

Council of Chief State School Officers. (2001). *CSSAP, Comprehensive social studies assessment project. Implementation guide for the social studies portfolio.* Washington, DC: Office of Education Research Inc.

Danielson, C. (1996). *Enhancing professional practice: A framework for teaching.* Alexandria, VA: Association for Supervision and Curriculum Development.

Dunn, R., & Dunn, K. (1992). *Teaching secondary students through their individual learning styles: Practical approaches for grades 7–12.* Boston: Allyn & Bacon.

Echevarria, J., Vogt, M., & Short, D. J. (2005). *Making content comprehensible for English learners: The SIOP model* (2nd ed.). Boston: Pearson Allyn and Bacon.

Educational Research Service. (1999). *Improving student achievement in social studies; Based on the handbook of research on improving student achievement* (2nd ed.). Arlington, VA: Author.

Engle, S. H., & Ochoa, A. S. (1988). *Education for democratic citizenship: Decision making in the social studies.* New York: Teachers College Press.

Epstein, J. (1997). *School, family, and community partnerships: Your handbook for action.* Thousand Oaks, CA: Corwin Press.

Erb, S., & Moore, N. (2003). A taste of Chautauqua: Historical investigation and oral presentation: Students study biographies to learn about a historical figure and make a presentation to the class portraying that individual. *Journal of Adolescent and Adult Literacy, 47,* 168–175.

Evans R., Newmann, F., & Saxe, D. (1996). Defining issues-centered education. In R. Evans & D. Saxe (Eds.), *Handbook on teaching social issues, NCSS Bulletin 93* (pp. 1–5). Washington, DC: National Council for the Social Studies.

Farris, P. J. (2005). *Elementary & middle school social studies: An interdisciplinary instructional approach* (3rd ed.). New York: McGraw-Hill.

Fine, M. (1995). *Habits of mind: Struggling over values in America's classrooms.* San Francisco: Jossey-Bass.

Gagné, R. N. (1970). *The conditions of learning.* New York: Holt, Rinehart & Winston.

Gallavan, N. P. (1997). Achieving civic competence through a DRAFT writing process. *Social Studies and the Young Learner, 10*(2), 14–16.

Gallavan, N. P. (2003). *What principals need to know about teaching . . . social studies.* New York: National Association of Elementary School Principals, Educational Research Services.

Gallavan, N. P. (in press). *Strengthening social studies education: Purposes, concepts, and strategies for middle school teachers and students.* Columbus, OH: Prentice Hall.

Gardner, H. (1983). *Frames of mind.* New York: Basic Books.

Hess, D. (2004). Discussion in social studies: Is it worth the trouble? *Social Education, 68*(2), 151–155.

Hess, D. (2005). How do teachers' political views influence teaching about controversial issues? *Social Education, 69*(1), 47–48.

Hoge, J. D., Field, S. L., Foster, S. J., & Nickell, P. (2004). *Real-world investigations for studies: Inquiries for middle and high school students based on the ten NCSS standards.* Upper Saddle River, NJ: Prentice Hall.

Hole, S., & McEntee, G. H. (1999). Reflection is at the heart of practice. *Educational Leadership, 56*(8), 34–37.

Howe, N., & Strauss, W. (2000). *Millennials rising: The next great generation.* New York: Vintage Books.

International Society for Technology in Education (2000). *National education standards for students: Connecting curriculum and technology.* Eugene, OR: ISTE.

Johnson, D. W., & Johnson, R. T. (1989). *Cooperation and competition: Theory and research.* Edina, MN: Interaction Book Company.

Jonson, K. (2002). *Being an effective mentor.* Thousand Oaks, CA: Corwin Press.

Joyce, B., & Weil, M. (1996). *Model of teachings* (5th ed.). Boston: Allyn and Bacon.

Kliebard, H. (1986). *The struggle for the American curriculum: 1893–1958.* Boston: Routledge and Kegan Paul.

Kohn, A. (1996). *Beyond discipline: From compliance to community.* Alexandria, VA: Association for Supervision and Curriculum Development.

Kohn, A. (1997). How not to teach values: A critical look at character education. *Phi Delta Kappan, 78*(6), 429–439.

Kottler, E., & Gallavan, N. P. (2007). *Secrets to success for beginning elementary school teachers.* Thousand Oaks, CA: Corwin Press.

Kottler, E., & Kottler, J. A. (2002). *Children with limited English: Teaching strategies for the regular classroom* (2nd ed.). Thousand Oaks, CA: Corwin Press.

Kottler, E., Kottler, J. A., & Kottler, C. J. (2004) *Secrets for secondary school teachers; How to succeed in your first year* (2nd ed.). Thousand Oaks, CA: Corwin Press.

Kottler, J. A., & Kottler, E. (2000). *Counseling skills for teachers.* Thousand Oaks, CA: Corwin Press.

Kottler, J. A., Zehm, S. J., & Kottler, E. (2005). *On being a teacher: The human dimension* (3rd ed.). Thousand Oaks, CA: Corwin Press.

Leming, J. S. (1985). Research on social studies curriculum and instruction: Interventions and outcome in the socio-moral domain. In W. B. Stanley (Ed.), *Review of research in social studies education: 1976–1982* (pp. 123–312). Washington, DC: National Council for the Social Studies.

Levstik, C., & Barton, K. (1997). *Doing history: Investigating with children in elementary and middle schools.* Mahwah, NJ: Erlbaum.

Lybarger, M. B. (1991). The historiography of social studies: Retrospect, circumspect, and prospect. In J. P. Shaver (Ed.), *Handbook of research on social studies reaching and learning* (pp. 3–15). New York: Macmillan.

Manning, M., Manning, G., & Long, R. (1994). *Theme immersion: Inquiry-based curriculum in elementary and middle schools.* Portsmouth, NH: Heinemann.

Martorella, P. (1994). *Social studies for elementary school children: Developing young citizens.* New York: Macmillan.

Marzano, R. J., & Kendall, J. S. (2007). *The new taxonomy of educational objectives* (2nd ed.). Thousand Oaks, CA: Corwin Press.

Marzano, R. J., Marzano, J. S., & Pickering, D. J. (2003). *Classroom management that works: Research-based strategies for every teacher.* Alexandria, VA: Association for Supervision and Curriculum Development.

Marzano, R., Pickering, D. J., & Pollack, J. E. (2001). *Classroom instruction that works: Research-based strategies for increasing student achievement.* Alexandria, VA: Association for Supervision and Curriculum Development.

Mason, C., Berson, M., Diem, R., Hicks, D., & Dralle, T. (2000). Guidelines for using technology to prepare social studies teachers. *Contemporary Issues in Technology and Teacher Education, 1*(1), 107–116.

Maxim, G. W. (2006). *Dynamic social studies for constructivist classrooms: Inspiring tomorrow's social scientists* (8th ed.). Upper Saddle River, NJ: Merrill Prentice Hall.

McCarthy, B. (1997). *4MAT course book* (Vol. 1, p. 61). Barrington, IL: EXCEL Inc.

Molebash, P., & Dodge, B. (2003). Kickstarting inquiry with Webquests and Web inquiry projects. *Social Education, 67*(3), 158–161.

National Council for Accreditation of Teacher Education. (1997). *Indicators of capabilities for teaching social studies.* Retrieved June 28, 2006, from http://www.ncate.org/ProgramStandards/NCSS/ncssmatrix.doc

National Council for the Social Studies. (1994). *Expectations of excellence: Curriculum standards for social studies.* Washington, DC: NCSS.

National Council for the Social Studies. (2006). Technology position statement and guidelines. *Social Education, 70*(5), 329–332.

Newmann, F. M. (1990). Higher-order thinking in teaching social studies: A rationale for the assessment of classroom thoughtfulness. *Journal of Curriculum Studies, 22,* 41–56.

Obenchain, K. M., & Morris, R. L. (2003). *50 social studies strategies for K–8 classrooms.* Upper Saddle River, NJ: Merrill Prentice Hall.

Pahl, R. H. (2005) *Creative ways to teach the mysteries of history.* Lanham, MD: Rowman & Littlefield Education.

Parker, W. C. (2005). *Social studies in elementary education.* Upper Saddle River, NJ: Prentice Hall.

Parker, W. C. (2006). Public discourse in schools: Purposes, problems, possibilities. *Educational Researcher, 35*(8), 11–18.

Portnor, H. (2002). *Mentoring new teachers.* Thousand Oaks, CA: Corwin Press.

Pultorak, E. G. (1993). Facilitating reflective thought in novice teachers. *Journal of Teacher Education, 44*(4), 288–295.

Readence, J. E., Bean, T. W., & Baldwin, R. S. (1998). Prereading strategies-anticipation guides. In *Content area literacy: An integrated approach* (6th ed., pp. 159–161). Dubuque, IA: Kendall/Hunt.

Risinger, C. F. (1996). Webbing the social studies: Using Internet and World Wide Web resources in social studies instruction. *Social Education, 60*(2), 111–112.

Schmoker, M. (2006). *Results now.* Alexandria, VA: Association for Supervision and Curriculum Development.

Schön, D. A. (1983). *The reflective practitioner: How professionals think in action.* New York: Basic Books.

Schug, M. C., Morton, J. S., & Wentworth, D. R. (1999). *Economics and the environment: Eco detectives.* Economics America, National Council on Economic Education.

Sheltered Instruction Observation Protocol. (2005). The SIOP Institute. Retrieved June 28, 2006, from http://www.siopinstitute.net/

Shermis, S. S. (1992). *Critical thinking: Helping students learn reflectively.* Bloomington, IN: ERIC Clearinghouse of Reading and Communication Skills.

Shulman, L. S. (1987). Knowledge and teaching: Foundations of the new reform. *Harvard Educational Review, 57,* 1–22.

Singleton, R. L. (2006). Preparing teachers to use simulations. *Trainers Times, 10*(1), 3–4.

Slavin, R. (1995). *Cooperative learning: Research, theory, and practice* (2nd ed.). Boston: Allyn & Bacon.

Stiggins, R. (2005). *Student-involved assessment FOR learning* (4th ed.). Upper Saddle River, NJ: Merrill Prentice Hall.

Street, C. (2002). The P.O.W.E.R. of process writing in content area classrooms. *Journal of Content Area Reading, 1,* 43–54.

Strong, W. (2006). *Write for insight: Empowering content area learning, grades 6-12.* Boston: Pearson Education, Inc.

Sunal, C. S., & Haas, M. E. (2002). *Social studies for elementary and middle grades: A constructivist approach.* Boston: Allyn and Bacon.

Taba, H. (1962). *Curriculum development: Theory and practice.* New York: Harcourt Brace.

Tomlinson, C. (1999). *The differentiated classroom: Responding to the needs of all learners.* Alexandria, VA: Association for Supervision and Curriculum Development.

Tomlinson, C.A., & McTighe, J. (2006). *Integrating differentiated instruction and understanding by design: Connecting content and kids.* Alexandria, VA: Association for Supervision and Curriculum Development.

Tyrone, R. M. (1934). *The social sciences as school subjects.* New York: Charles Scribner's Sons.

Van Manen, M. (1977). Linking ways of knowing with ways of being practical. *Curriculum Inquiry, 6,* 205–228.

Vygotsky, L. S. (1978). *Mind in society: The development of higher psychological processes.* Cambridge, MA: Harvard University Press.

Wallis, C., & Steptoe, S. (2006, December 18). How to bring our schools out of the 20th century. *Time,* 50–56.

Wiggins, G., & McTighe, J. (2006). *Understanding by design* (Expanded 2nd ed.). Upper Saddle River, NJ: Pearson Education.

Wink, J. (2004). *Critical pedagogy: Notes from the real world* (3rd ed.). New York: Addison Wesley Longman.

Yildirim, A. (2003). Instructional planning in a centralized school system: Lessons of a study among primary school teachers in Turkey. *International Review of Education, 49*(5), 525–543.

Ziechner, M. K., & Liston, D. P. (1987). Teaching student teachers to reflect. *Harvard Educational Review, 57*(1), 23–48.

Zinsser, W. (1988). *Writing to learn.* New York: Harper and Row.

Index

CORWIN PRESS

The Corwin Press logo—a raven striding across an open book—represents the union of courage and learning. Corwin Press is committed to improving education for all learners by publishing books and other professional development resources for those serving the field of PreK–12 education. By providing practical, hands-on materials, Corwin Press continues to carry out the promise of its motto: **"Helping Educators Do Their Work Better."**

DATE DUE